MW00579746

"Appealing to ancient and contemporary poets and writers, complemented by the insights of theologians and biblical scholars, *Creation Is Groaning* captures the wonder, beauty, and suffering of creation and invites readers to enter deeply into the heart of God, the heart of Christ, and the heart of the entire cosmos. The theological, Christological, biblical, ethical, and ecological links made throughout this edited volume create a rich tapestry of thought that challenges basic assumptions and definitions while opening doors to new ways of seeing and living life in a sacred universe."

—Carol J. Dempsey, OP
University of Portland
Oregon

"Each new age interprets its religious tradition through lenses that are central to that age. Ecosensitivity is a prominent lens for our age. Within the recent past, various hermeneutical approaches attentive to this lens have developed. This collection of essays produced by six prominent Australian theologians partner ecosensitivity with the theological themes of incarnation and promise. The end product of such creative rethinking is a set of essays that offer new insights into the inherited religious tradition and new challenges for living in the contemporary world."

—Dianne Bergant, CSA
Professor of Old Testament Studies
Catholic Theological Union
Chicago, Illinois

Creation Is Groaning

Biblical and Theological Perspectives

Edited by
Mary L. Coloe, PBVM

A Michael Glazier Book

LITURGICAL PRESS
Collegeville, Minnesota

www.litpress.org

A Michael Glazier Book published by Liturgical Press

Cover design by Jodi Hendrickson. Cover image: Thinkstock.

1	2	3	4	5	6	7	8	9

Library of Congress Cataloging-in-Publication Data

Creation is groaning : Biblical and theological perspectives / edited by Mary L. Coloe, PBVM.
      pages   cm
   "A Michael Glazier book."
   Includes bibliographical references and index.
   ISBN 978-0-8146-8065-0 (pbk. : alk. paper) — ISBN 978-0-8146-8090-2 (e-book)
   1. Creation—Biblical teaching.   2. Creationism.   3. Catholic Church—Doctrines.   I. Coloe, Mary L., 1949– editor of compilation.

BS651.C694   2013
231.7'65—dc23   2013007279

Contents

Preface   vii

Journal Abbreviations   xi

List of Contributors   xii

1. Creation Seen in the Light of Christ: A Theological Sketch   1
   Denis Edwards

2. Subdue and Conquer: An Ecological Perspective
   on Genesis 1:28   19
   Antoinette Collins

3. If Not Now, When? The Ecological Potential
   of Isaiah's "New Things"   33
   Dermot Nestor

4. The Liberation of Creation: Romans 8:11-29   57
   Marie Turner

5. Creation in the Gospel of John   71
   Mary L. Coloe

6. Christ and Creation: Logos and Cosmos   91
   Anthony J. Kelly

Bibliography   117

Author Index   129

Preface

In recent years, as biblical scholars have engaged with current ecological challenges, two major hermeneutical projects have emerged. The Earth Bible project, under the leadership of Norman Habel from Adelaide, Australia, has proposed a way of reading the biblical texts according to six principles of eco-justice: the principle of intrinsic worth, the principle of interconnectedness, the principle of voice, the principle of purpose, the principle of mutual custodianship, the principle of resistance.[1] As is clear from this list, this project reads the Bible from the perspective of Earth. The second hermeneutical approach is led by David Horrell from the University of Exeter. The Exeter project takes a more explicitly theological approach to biblical interpretation and suggests a critical engagement with the text through particular doctrinal lenses such as the goodness of all creation; humanity as part of the community of creation; interconnectedness in failure and flourishing; the covenant with all creation; creation's calling to praise God; liberation and reconciliation for all things.[2] These two approaches are not necessarily conflicting,

1. These principles are elaborated on in Earth Bible Team, "Guiding Ecojustice Principles," chap. 2 in *Readings from the Perspective of Earth*, ed. Norman C. Habel, The Earth Bible 1 (Sheffield, UK: Sheffield Academic Press, 2000).

2. These hermeneutical lenses are elaborated on in David G. Horrell, *The Bible and the Environment: Towards a Critical Ecological Biblical Theology; Biblical Challenges in the Contemporary World* (London: Equinox, 2010), 129-36. David Horrell acknowledges the significance of the interpretive work of Ernst Conradie whose approach can be found in Ernst M. Conradie, "What on Earth Is an Ecological Hermeneutics [sic]?: Some Broad Parameters," in *Ecological Hermeneutics: Biblical, Historical and Theological Perspectives*, ed. David G. Horrell, et al. (London: T & T Clark, 2010).

viii Creation Is Groaning

and together they can provide a critical Christian hermeneutic that is both theological and ecological.

In commenting on the Earth Bible principles, Dianne Jacobson suggested two additional theological principles: the principles of incarnation and promise.[3] These two principles offer what the Exeter project considers to be doctrinal lenses that recognize the significance of the biblical text as Scripture that has shaped and guided the Christian tradition. The essays in this volume address these principles of incarnation and promise. They begin from a premise that the *Logos* of God, who called creation into being, became human in the life of Jesus of Nazareth, and through his rising reveals the promise of creation's fulfillment.

The volume begins and ends with essays by two foremost Australian theologians, Denis Edwards and Anthony Kelly. Both address the centrality of the Christ event and its meaning for developing a Christian ecological theology, spirituality, and ethic.

Denis Edwards takes as his starting point the resurrection before moving to propose a unified understanding of creation and incarnation as one act of love, then outlines four characteristics of creation in the light of Christ—as enabling creaturely autonomy, empowering evolutionary emergence, accepting the limits of creaturely processes, and suffering with suffering creation. Tony Kelly begins his essay with a theological reflection based on the prologue of John's gospel, which holds together *Logos* and *Cosmos*. He then addresses the possible rhetoric that may assist theological reflection today in its task of speaking about God, creation, and Jesus against a backdrop of our current understanding of an evolving universe. He explores the rhetoric of fulfillment, participation, and cosmic extension.

Between these two essays by systematic theologians, four biblical scholars and theologians address particular scriptural texts that are significant in ecological conversations.

Antoinette Collins examines the highly problematic text of Genesis 1:28 with its language of "subdue and conquer." Her work traces the developing interpretive tradition of the original Hebrew

---

3. Earth Bible Team, "Conversations with Gene Tucker and Other Writers," in *The Earth Story in Genesis*, ed. Norman C. Habel and Shirley Wurst, The Earth Bible 2 (Sheffield, UK: Sheffield Academic Press, 2000), 32.

words as they are rendered in the later Greek, Aramaic, and Latin translations. She then offers three contextual interpretative approaches to this text: in the context of humanity made in God's image; in the context of an Earth-centered narrative; and in the context of Australian Aboriginal praxis.

During the experience of Exile, the prophet Isaiah held out the promise of a return to Jerusalem. An aspect of his prophetic imagination is his use of creation symbolism to speak not only of a New Exodus but also of the re-creating of a new people. Dermot Nestor examines this creation symbolism, considering if it may offer a source for ecological reflection in our own time. He examines how Isaiah's eschatological vision looks to the transformation of both the human and nonhuman creation joined in praise of God.

Eschatological promise comes to the fore in the following essay by Marie Turner who examines the liberating potential of Romans 8:11-19. Drawing on both the Pauline text and its resonances in the Wisdom of Solomon, Turner describes a vision of all creation, human and nonhuman, caught up together in the triumph of the risen Christ over death. All creation groans in the labor of bringing to birth the new potentialities of the resurrection.

The final biblical essay is by Mary Coloe who proposes that a theology of creation pervades the entire Gospel of John. She examines the beginning of the gospel and its relationship to Genesis 1, and the passion narrative and its echoes of Genesis 2. Her exegetical examination of the beginning and ending of the gospel leads to a consideration of some theological implications such as the cosmic dimensions of the incarnation and the Johannine presentation of salvation as re-creation.

This research and the resulting publication would not have been possible except for the generous grant from the Australian Catholic University. On behalf of all contributors, I thank the research committees within the university and the faculty of theology and philosophy for supporting this project.

Hans Christoffersen from Liturgical Press has also been most supportive and understanding of the aims of the project and the challenges to be addressed in order to bring ideas into essays and into a published volume. Thanks to all at Liturgical Press for their expertise and show of faith.

In the final tasks of editing this volume, I was fortunate to take some sabbatical time at "The Archer," a creation spirituality center near Brisbane. Here, I was nourished by the beauty of the Australian bush and by a community whose way of living embodied respectful, nurturing relationships with Earth and all her creatures: walking, hopping, climbing, sliding, crawling, swimming, and flying. Thank you, Elaine, Tony, Ian, and Tilde.

Journal Abbreviations

ABR   Australian Biblical Review
CBQ   Catholic Biblical Quarterly
JBL   Journal of Biblical Literature
JSNT   Journal for the Study of the New Testament
JTS   Journal of Theological Studies
NTS   New Testament Studies
SCE   Studies in Christian Ethics
SJT   Scottish Journal of Theology
TLZ   Theologische Literaturzeitung

Contributors

Antoinette Collins lectures in Old Testament studies at Australian Catholic University in Sydney.

Mary L. Coloe is an associate professor and lectures in New Testament studies at Australian Catholic University in Melbourne.

Denis Edwards is associate professor in systematic theology at Flinders University and Catholic Theological College of South Australia. He is also an adjunct lecturer in theology at Australian Catholic University.

Anthony J. Kelly is professor of theology at Australian Catholic University and deputy director of the university's Institute for Catholic Identity and Mission. He has been a member of the Vatican's International Theological Commission since 2004.

Dermot Nestor is head of the School of Theology at Australian Catholic University and lectures in Old Testament studies in Sydney.

Marie Turner is a senior lecturer in biblical studies at Flinders University in Adelaide, South Australia, and adjunct lecturer at Australian Catholic University.

Chapter 1

Creation Seen in the Light of Christ: A Theological Sketch

Denis Edwards

Is there anything specific to the Christian understanding of creation? Christianity certainly shares with Judaism, and with Islam, a great deal. From the ancient faith of Israel, it learns that there is only one transcendent God who is Creator of absolutely everything; that this transcendent God is immanently present to all creatures; that this God not only creates things in the beginning but is their constant source of existence, life, and fruitfulness; that this Creator delights in the goodness of creation; that the fruitfulness of creation is a result of divine blessing; that humans are uniquely made in the image of God (Gen 1:1-31).

The common biblical tradition teaches that human beings are called to till and to take care of creation (Gen 2:15), that human sin damages creation, but that God, nevertheless, commits God's self to creation by an everlasting covenant (Gen 9:8-17). It sees humans as standing before a Creator, and a creation, far greater than anything humans can grasp, as called to cosmic humility and to the recognition that other creatures have their own proper relationship to their Creator not mediated by human beings (Job 38:39-12). This same ancient biblical tradition locates human beings within an interrelated community of creation, a community of praise and thanksgiving (Pss 104, 148; Dan 3:51-90).[1]

All this and much more belong to the common biblical tradition. What then is specific to the Christian view of creation? In what follows I will attempt a partial response to this question: first, by proposing that the Christian theology of creation begins from the resurrection of the crucified one; second, by arguing that creation and incarnation can be understood as united in one divine act of self-giving love; third, by outlining four characteristics of creation understood in the light of Christ—as enabling creaturely autonomy, empowering evolutionary emergence, accepting the limits of creaturely processes, and suffering with suffering creation; fourth, by suggesting that in spite of all ambiguity in our experience of the natural world, the revelation of God in Christ enables us to claim that creation is an act of divine love.

1. Beginning from the Resurrection of the Crucified Jesus

A specifically Christian theology of creation begins only with the resurrection of Jesus. Those who had loved Jesus in his lifetime, investing all their religious hopes in him and leaving all to follow him, caught up in his vision and in his person, had lost everything in his condemnation and death on a Roman cross. For Peter, Mary Magdalene, and the other disciples to meet Jesus risen from the dead and transformed in the glory of God was a radically new experience of forgiveness, peace, and hope. In the Risen One, they knew God. In the transfigured Jesus, the fullness of God was revealed. In Jesus, they experienced the boundless love of God and were caught up in a joy that echoes through the centuries in the life of the church.

In some way they knew then that all sin, all the violence of the world, and death itself were transformed by God's saving act. They experienced themselves as brought from death to wonderful new life, participating in the life of the risen Christ by the Spirit of God. For them God would forever be God revealed in Jesus and in the

---

1. This biblical line of thought has been explored by Richard Bauckham in his *The Bible and Ecology: Rediscovering the Community of Creation* (London: Darton, Longman & Todd, 2010), 37–102.

Holy Spirit given in his name. The crucified and risen Jesus would be forever the human face of God.

Jesus, in his life and even in his death, above all in his death, is revealed as "God is with us" (Matt 1:23). Jesus' cruel, ugly death now becomes the radical sign of hope, the unthinkable expression of divine forgiveness and love without limits. And it becomes the expression of God-with-us and the promise of life in all our experiences of suffering, no matter how devastating. The disciples saw the light of God in the Risen One, and they knew his divinity in a way not possible during his lifetime.

The disciples of Jesus had to find words to speak of what was beyond words. They needed ways to express what they knew in the risen Christ, that he is from God the Creator, that he is this God-with-us. They found a fruitful insight in the biblical concept of Wisdom—a deeply traditional way of speaking of God's presence and action. In the biblical tradition, Wisdom (Gk. *Sophia*) is personified as God's companion in the creating and sustaining of all things (Prov 8:22-31; Sir 24:3-7; Wis 8:1-4). This ever-creative Wisdom of God comes to live with human beings. She makes her home among them and invites them to come to her table to share the food and drink she provides (Prov 9:1-6; Sir 24:8-22; Wis 8:16-21).

Jewish thinkers could see Wisdom come to us as Torah (Sir 24:23). The early Christians, in the light of the resurrection, saw Jesus as the Wisdom of God come to us in the flesh. *Sophia*, the one through whom everything in the universe is created, has now come to be with us in Jesus. The fullness of God's Wisdom is revealed in the human face of Jesus, in his life and ministry, in his death and resurrection. Paul, a Pharisee learned in the ways of Judaism, tells us that it is Christ crucified who is the power and Wisdom of God (1 Cor 1:24), and he can say that everything is created in Christ (1 Cor 4:6). In John we find that, like Wisdom who comes from God to feed us at her table, Jesus-Wisdom feeds the five thousand on the mountainside; he himself is the very bread of life, that living bread that comes down from heaven to give life to the world (John 6:5).[2]

2. On the Wisdom theme in John 6, see André Feuillet, *Johannine Studies* (Staten Island, NY: Alba House, 1964), 76–102.

A Jewish writer, like Philo of Alexandria, could use both Wisdom (*Sophia*) and Word (*Logos*) language to speak of God's creating and revealing presence. So in New Testament hymns, such as the prologue of John's gospel and the opening of Hebrews, we find Christ as the Word of God, in texts with a Wisdom structure of thought and in language that echoes biblical Wisdom hymns (John 1:1-14; Heb 1:1-3). For John, Jesus is clearly and unambiguously the creative Wisdom/Word of God—"all things came into being through him" (John 1:3)—now made flesh in our midst. In the late Pauline corpus, Christ is understood, like Wisdom, as the one in whom all things are created, the one in whom all things hold together, and, as "the firstborn from the dead," the one in whom all will be reconciled (Col 1:15-20) and recapitulated (Eph 1:20-22).

In this New Testament theology, there is an inner relationship between creation and incarnation. Everything in the universe is created by God through the eternal Wisdom/Word of God. This Wisdom/Word of God is made flesh in Jesus in order that the whole creation might participate with human beings in the salvation and fulfillment of all things promised in the resurrection of Jesus. Early theologians, like Athanasius, see Christ as the one true Word, Wisdom, and Radiance of God made flesh.[3] He writes of John 1:3 as the "all-inclusive" text: "All things came into being through him, and without him not one thing came into being."[4] He sees the Word of creation as becoming flesh in order that humanity might be deified, transformed by grace so that it might partake in the divine life of the Trinity. In his anti-Arian writings, he uses frequently both the verb *theopoieō* and the noun he coins, *theopoiēsis*, to defend the eternal divinity and divine condescension of the Word, who is made flesh to bring about our deification: "So he was not a human being and later became God. But, being God, he later became a human being in order that we may be deified."[5]

---

3. Athanasius, *Orations against the Arians* 1:46, translated in Khaled Anatolios, *Athanasius* (London and New York: Routledge, 2004), 103.

4. Athanasius, *On the Incarnation* 2, translated in R. W. Thompson, *Athanasius, Contra Gentes and de Incarnatione* (Oxford: Clarendon Press, 1971), 139.

5. *Orations against the Arians* 63, translated in Anatolios, *Athanasius*, 96.

The Word/Wisdom of God is made flesh for the deifying trans-formation of human creatures and with them of the whole universe of creatures. So Athanasius writes of the Father's love for humanity, "on account of which he not only gave consistence to all things in his Word but brought it about that the creation itself, of which the apostle says that it 'awaits the revelation of the children of God,' will at a certain point be delivered 'from the bondage of corruption into the glorious freedom of the children of God' (Rom 8:19-21)."[6]

2. Creation and Incarnation: God's Self-Bestowal

Is there a way of summing up in a few words what is most central to the specifically Christian view of God? With Karl Rahner, I see the concept of divine self-communication, or divine self-bestowal, as an encapsulation of what God does for us in Christ and the Spirit.[7] The Christian experience is fundamentally of a God who gives God's self to us in two ways:

1. God gives God's very self explicitly and irrevocably to crea-tures in the humanity of Jesus, in all that makes up his life, death, and resurrection.
2. This same God gives God's self to creatures in the Holy Spirit in the free and abundant gift of grace and, in the Pen-tecostal experience, constitutes the community of disciples into the church of Jesus Christ.

God gives God's self to us in the Word made flesh and in the Spirit poured out in grace. Paul speaks of two divine "sendings": "But when the fullness of time had come, God sent his Son, born of a woman, born under the law, in order to redeem those who were under the law, so that we might receive adoption as children. And because you are children, God has sent the Spirit of his Son into our hearts, crying, 'Abba! Father!' So you are no longer a slave but a child, and if a child then also an heir, through God" (Gal 4:4-5). The concept

6. Ibid., 157.
7. See, for example, Karl Rahner, *Foundations of Christian Faith: An Introduction to the Idea of Christianity* (New York: Seabury Press, 1978), 136.

of divine self-bestowal in Word and Spirit can be seen as a brief summary of the central doctrines of Christian faith: of Christology, pneumatology, and trinitarian theology. It expresses what we experience of God in the economy of salvation and, because God is faithful, we rightly hold that the God we experience in our history, as giving God's self to us in the Word made flesh and the Spirit poured out, represents the true nature of God as Trinity.

What is revealed in the Christ-event is a God who gives God's self to creatures. Based on this revelation in Christ, Karl Rahner sees divine self-bestowal as defining every aspect of God's action, in creation, redemption in Christ, and final fulfillment.[8] He sees creation itself as an act of self-giving love that reaches its goal only in the self-giving of the incarnation and in the final transformation of all things in the risen Christ. The creation of the universe of creatures is the first element in the free and radical decision of God to give God's self in love to that which is not divine; when God freely chose to bestow God's self in love, creation came to be as the addressee of this self-bestowal.

This means that God's self-giving in Christ is the real foundation of the history of the natural world. The mystery of God's will, we are told in Ephesians, has been revealed to us "according to his good pleasure that he set forth in Christ, as a plan for the fullness of time, to gather up all things in him, things in heaven and things on earth" (Eph 1:9-10). It is not simply that the event of Jesus Christ unfolds against the background of nature. The story of the natural world, and everything that science can tell us about its evolution, is part of a larger vision of divine self-bestowal.[9] The big bang and the expansion of our universe from a small, dense, hot state 13.7 billion years ago, and the evolution of life since its beginning on Earth 3.7 billion years ago—this whole story exists *within* the vision of the divine purpose.

Harvey Egan has said that the briefest possible summary of Rahner's theological enterprise in found is "his creative appropriation of

8. Karl Rahner, "Christology in the Setting of Modern Man's Understanding of Himself and of His World," in *Theological Investigations* 11 (New York: Seabury Press, 1974), 219.

9. Karl Rahner, "Resurrection: Section D. Theology," in *Encyclopedia of Theology: A Concise Sacramentum Mundi* (London: Burns and Oates, 1975), 1442.

Scotus's view that God creates in order to communicate *self* and that creation exists in order to be the recipient of God's free gift of self."[10] While one line of Christian theology has held that the incarnation comes about simply as a remedy for sin, another, associated in Eastern Christianity, particularly with Maximus the Confessor (580–662), and in Western theology with Franciscan theology, exemplified in Duns Scotus (1266–1308), sees the incarnation as always the divine intention in the creation of a universe of creatures.

The incarnation, then, is not simply a remedy for sin or a corrective for a creation that has gone wrong. Once sin exists, of course, the incarnation expresses divine forgiveness in a most beautiful and radical way, but the incarnation is not something added on to creation; it is not a kind of backup plan. The incarnation is the meaning of creation. God freely chooses, from the beginning, to create a world in which the Word would be made flesh and the Spirit poured out.[11] The incarnation expresses the divine purpose in creating, which is the divine self-bestowal. Creation and incarnation are united in the one act of God: they are "two moments and two phases of the *one* process of God's self-giving and self-expression, although it is an intrinsically differentiated process."[12] The creation of the universe and all of its creatures and the incarnation are to be seen as distinct dimensions of the one act of divine self-bestowal in love. In the next three sections, I will explore briefly three characteristics of God's creative act understood as divine self-giving.

3. Enabling Creaturely Autonomy

How should we think of the Creator's interrelationship with the world of creatures? Are we to think of God as constantly intervening in the laws and conditions of the natural world (sometimes called "occasionalism") or as intervening at certain points in the process

10. Harvey D. Egan, "Theology and Spirituality," in *The Cambridge Companion to Karl Rahner*, ed. Declan Marmion and Mary E. Hines (Cambridge, UK: Cambridge University Press, 2005), 16.

11. Karl Rahner, "Christology within an Evolutionary View of the World," in *Theological Investigations* 5 (Baltimore: Helicon Press, 1966), 184–87.

12. Rahner, *Foundations*, 197.

of evolution (as proponents of "intelligent design" seem to think)? Or are we to think of God as setting the processes of the natural world in place and then allowing things to run their course (the position of "deism")? Thomas Aquinas offers a far richer theology of creation than either interventionism or deism; I see Aquinas's response as a fundamental basis for contemporary dialogue between science and theology, with his metaphysical understanding of the relationship between primary and secondary causality.

Primary causality for Aquinas is simply God's creative act that enables all creatures to exist and to act. God is unlike all creatures, in that it is God's very nature to exist. The One whose nature is to exist causes existence (*esse*) in all other things. Creation is the interior relationship between the Creator and each creature by which the creature is held in being. If God were not interiorly present to each creature enabling it to be, it would be nothing. Aquinas sees all things in the universe existing in the community of creation only as created by God *ex nihilo* at each moment and as dependent on God entirely for their existence and action at every point. He sees God's providence as governing all creation to its final end, which is participation in the goodness of God. To speak of God's creative act as primary cause is to use the word *cause* in an analogical fashion. God's creative act is radically unlike creaturely causality, radically beyond empirical observation, and radically beyond human comprehension.

In Aquinas's thought, all the interacting agents at work in the empirical world are seen as secondary causes. This includes literally everything that can be studied by the natural and social sciences. God as primary cause is always and everywhere creatively and providentially at work in all creaturely interactions, in all the conditions, constants, contingencies, and laws of the natural world. God is not a cause like creaturely causes in the world and is never to be thought of as one amongst such causes. God acts creatively in and through creatures that are themselves truly causal. Aquinas sees the Creator as respecting the proper dignity of created causes because of "the abundance of his goodness imparting to creatures also the dignity of causing."[13]

13. Thomas Aquinas, *Summa Theologiae*, Ia, q. 22, a. 3, trans. by Thomas Gilby, *St Thomas Aquinas Summa Theologiae*, vol. 5 (Cambridge, UK: Blackfriars, 1967), 99.

God's respect for creation's autonomy is such that God wants creation to have its own pattern of causality. Aquinas's theology leads to a genuine respect for the proper integrity and independence of the natural sciences. There is never a resort to the "God of the gaps" to solve a scientific problem. One who follows Aquinas would not be inclined to search for a place where God intervenes in creation because God is found in every dimension of creation: God "acts interiorly in all things," because "God is properly the universal cause of *esse*, which is innermost in all things."[14]

The divine act of creation is unique. On the one hand, creation is a relationship of absolute nearness and real dependence, where each creature is dependent on God for its existence and capacity to act. On the other hand, God establishes the creature in genuine difference from God's self, and in the relationship of creation—because of God's love and respect for creatures—each creature has its own otherness, integrity, and proper autonomy.

A fundamental principle of this relationship, one grounded in Aquinas's thought and often articulated by Karl Rahner, is expressed in the axiom: radical dependence on God and the genuine autonomy of the creature are directly and not inversely related.[15] In everyday experience it seems that the more one thing depends on another, the less autonomy it has. The relationship of creation is the opposite: the closer creatures are to God, the more they can be truly themselves. We humans know this from the experience of grace: the closer we are drawn into the love of God, the freer we are. In relation to God, "radical dependence grounds autonomy."[16] Creaturely integrity is not diminished because a creature's existence is dependent on God but flourishes precisely in this dependence. This is true not only in the divine relationship to human beings but also in God's interaction with all the dynamics of the natural world, including the emergence of our universe and the evolution of life on Earth.

14. Aquinas, *Summa Theologiae*, Ia, q. 105, a. 6, trans. by T. C. O'Brien, *St Thomas Aquinas Summa Theologiae*, vol. 14 (Cambridge, UK: Blackfriars, 1975), 79.

15. See, for example, Rahner, *Foundations*, 78–79.

16. Ibid., 79.

4. *Empowering Evolutionary Emergence*

One of the radical changes in our view of reality, since the time of Aquinas, springs from the nineteenth-century discovery by Charles Darwin and Alfred Russel Wallace not only of the large-scale evolution of life on our planet but also of the fundamental role played by natural selection in the evolutionary emergence of insects, eagles, whales, and human beings, and of their wings, eyes, and brains. Then, in the twentieth century, building on Albert Einstein's general relativity and the astronomical observations of Edwin Hubble, cosmologists discovered that the universe is not static but dynamic and expanding, and that it has emerged from an unthinkable small, hot, and dense state over the last 13.7 billion years.

How is this dynamic, evolutionary understanding of reality to be understood in relationship to God's creative act? In Aquinas's view, God's creative act sustains all creatures in existence (*conservatio*) and enables them to act (*concursus*). Clearly in the light of insights into the emergent nature of reality, Aquinas's view needs further development. It needs to be a theology of God's creative act as enabling and empowering the evolutionary becoming of the interconnected world of creatures. This task was taken up by Karl Rahner. He saw the need for a theology of creation that can account for the emergence of the new, as in the transitions from inert matter to living creatures, and from living creatures to self-conscious human beings.

Rahner sees the self-bestowal of the transcendent God as "the most immanent factor in the creature."[17] What is the effect of this presence of God? A fundamental effect of God's creative self-giving presence, Rahner holds, is that creation itself has the capacity for emergence, to become more, to become what is new. Rahner calls this dynamic capacity for the new "self-transcendence." The two concepts of divine self-bestowal and creaturely self-transcendence are interrelated: it is God's self-bestowal that enables and empowers creaturely self-transcendence. This means that God's creative, immanent presence to all things not only enables them to exist, and to act, as theologians like Aquinas taught, but also to evolve into the

---

17. Rahner, "Immanent and Transcendent Consummation of the World," in *Theological Investigations* 10 (London: Darton, Longman & Todd), 281.

new. This idea of creaturely self-transcendence is worked out in Rahner's anthropology and in his evolutionary Christology, but it plays a fundamental systematic role in many aspects of his theological work.[18]

The "self" in self-transcendence means that the evolutionary capacity is truly intrinsic to creaturely reality. It comes from within the natural world. This means that the emergence of the new is completely open to explanation at the scientific level. God's creative presence operates at a strictly metaphysical and theological level. Just as God's creative act enables creatures to exist, so this same creative presence of God enables the new to emerge from within the natural world itself, according to the natural world's own processes and laws. Emergence is a creaturely reality, but it exists only because of God's creative act. God's presence in self-bestowing love enables creatures to exist, to interact, and to evolve.

Rahner links this pattern of self-transcendence to Christology, seeing Jesus Christ as both God's self-bestowal in the Word made flesh to the universe of creatures and, in his humanity, as the self-transcendence of the created universe to God. I believe it needs to be linked more fully to pneumatology as well, so that the emergence of the new, as when life first appears in a lifeless universe, can be seen as given through the Word and in the Holy Spirit. As Athanasius says, "The Father creates and renews all things through the Word and in the Spirit."[19] He sees the Spirit as the one who "binds creation to the Word."[20] Much more recently, Walter Kasper has written of the Creator Spirit:

> Since the Spirit is divine love in person, he is, first of all, the source of creation, for creation is the overflow of God's love and a participation in God's being. The Holy Spirit is the internal (in God) presupposition of communicability of God

18. See, for example, Rahner's *Hominisation: The Evolutionary Origin of Man as a Theological Problem* (London: Burns and Oates, 1965); "Christology within an Evolutionary View of the World," in *Theological Investigations* 5 (Baltimore: Helicon, 1966); "Immanent and Transcendent Consummation," 273–89; and various passages in his *Foundations*.

19. Athanasius, *Serapion* 1:24, in Anatolios, *Athanasius*, 224.

20. Ibid., 225.

outside of himself. But the Spirit is also the source of movement and life in the created world. Whenever something new
arises, whenever life is awakened and reality reaches ecstati-
cally beyond itself, in all seeking and striving, in every ferment
and birth, and even more in the beauty of creation, something
of the being and activity of God's Spirit is manifested.[21]

The Spirit of God is the Life-Giver who enables and empowers
the emergence of galaxies and stars, the Sun, and its solar system,
with Earth placed at the right distance from the Sun to enable life:
the first forms of prokaryotic life; more complex life forms; the ex-
traordinary flourishing of sea creatures; flowering trees and shrubs;
the diversity of land animals, mammals, and human beings with
their extraordinarily complex brains. God's presence through the
Word and in the Spirit enables the universe of creatures to exist, to
interact, and to evolve within the one community of life on Earth
within a dynamic, evolutionary universe. God seems prepared to
create through long, complex processes of emergence, respecting
the processes, rather than through constant intervention. How might
we think theologically of the power of God at work in all of this?

5. Accepting the Limits of Creaturely Processes

In the Christ-event, self-giving love is revealed as the way of God.
The incarnation and, above all, the cross of Jesus reveal a God who
enters into the vulnerability of love in a kenotic way (Phil 2:7). Paul
sees Christ crucified as the very "power of God and the wisdom of
God" (1 Cor 1:24). For Christian theology, the absolutely vulnerable
human being on the cross is the true revelation of God. As Walter
Kasper has said, in the extreme vulnerability of the cross we do not
find the loss of divinity, nor the absence of divinity, but the true
revelation of divinity.[22] In Jesus crucified, divine power is revealed
as the boundless power of unthinkable love. It is revealed as the
omnipotence of love. The power of God revealed in the cross is not
a power to dominate but a power-in-love.

---

21. Walter Kasper, *The God of Jesus Christ* (London: SCM, 1983), 227.
22. Ibid., 195.

The resurrection of the Crucified reveals the power of this divine love to heal, liberate, and bring creation to transfigured new life. Divine power-in-love is capable not only of the vulnerability of the cross but also of bringing forgiveness, participation in divine life, and resurrection life to human beings. The resurrection promises fulfillment to the whole interconnected creation (Rom 8:19-25). To believe in God as all-powerful is to believe in the omnipotence of divine love and its eschatological victory over sin, violence, and death. The vulnerable self-giving love of Christ gives expression in our finite, creaturely world to the divine nature. This self-bestowing love, revealed in Jesus' life and death and culminating in the transforming power of the resurrection, is the true icon of the Triune God in our world and the true revelation of divine omnipotence.

This same pattern of divine power-in-love discovered in the Christ-event can be read back into the divine act of creating a universe of creatures. Power-in-love can be thought of as characterizing the whole divine act of creation, God's original creation, God's ongoing creative act, and God's eschatological fulfillment of creation. In all of this, God freely creates in a way that respects the limits and integrity of creaturely processes. This means that we can think of God as waiting upon the proper evolutionary unfolding of these finite processes.

In his late work, Edward Schillebeeckx has written on the defenselessness and vulnerability of God. He discusses this divine vulnerability at three levels: God's defenselessness in creation, God's defenselessness in Jesus Christ, and the Holy Spirit's defenselessness in the church and in the world.[23] He explains that he speaks of the defenselessness of God rather than of divine powerlessness, because powerlessness and power contradict one another, whereas defenselessness and power need not: "We know from experience that those who make themselves vulnerable can sometimes disarm evil!"[24] In creation, he sees a kind of divine yielding on God's part as God makes room for the other, and in creating human beings, God makes

23. Edward Schillebeeckx, *For the Sake of the Gospel* (New York: Crossroad, 1990), 88–102.

24. Edward Schillebeeckx, *Church: The Human Story of God* (New York: Crossroad, 1990), 90.

God's self vulnerable to human freedom. Schillebeeckx sees God's act of creation as "an adventure, full of risks."[25] This does not do away with divine creative and saving power. This creative power, however, does not break into creation from outside. It comes from within creation and shows itself as "the power of love which challenges, gives life and frees human beings."[26]

To say that God waits upon creatures is not to suggest that God is simply allowing things to run their course. God was with Jesus in his cross, holding him in love, and acting powerfully in the Spirit, transforming evil and death into the source of healing for the world. In creation, too, divine power can be seen as the transcendent power-in-love that has an unimaginable capacity to respect the autonomy and independence of creatures, to work with them patiently, and to bring them to their fulfillment. This is not divine passivity but the creative and powerful waiting on another. God works with creaturely limits and waits upon them with infinite patience. By creating in love, God freely accepts the limitations of working with finite creatures.

Based upon the incarnation and the cross of Christ, it can be said that there may be circumstances when God freely accepts the limitations of creating in and through finite entities and processes, because of God's love and respect for finite creatures and for creaturely processes. God achieves the divine purposes, not in ways that override the proper autonomy of creaturely processes, but by an infinite power-in-love that lives within the process and accompanies creation in love, promising to bring it to healing and fulfillment in Christ.

6. Suffering with Suffering Creation

Evolution is a costly process, involving not only cooperation and symbiosis but also creatures preying on other creatures and competing for resources. Random mutations provide novelty that enables evolutionary emergence, but they more often bring damage and suffering. Death is intrinsic to the pattern of evolutionary emergence that can occur only through a series of generations. The costs of evolution, and above all the terrible costs of human violence, have

25. Ibid.
26. Ibid., 91.

raised important theological questions not only about God's power but also about God's engagement with the suffering of creatures.

Does God suffer with suffering creatures? For thinkers like Irenaeus and Athanasius, the concept of divine impassibility defends the biblical and Christian concept of the radical transcendence of God and does this precisely in opposition to Hellenistic views. At the center of their thought is the Christian concept of *creatio ex nihilo*. Because God is radically other than all creatures, God can enable the whole world of creatures to exist constantly and faithfully. God's impassibility defends divine otherness against tendencies to see God as trapped within the vicissitudes of creation, as at the mercy of changing human emotions, or as arbitrary and fickle like pagan gods or human tyrants. It points to the constancy and fidelity of divine love in creation, salvation, and final fulfillment.

These are fundamentals of Christian theology that must, and can, be safeguarded, I believe, in a contemporary theology of a God who suffers with suffering creation. The way forward is by reflection on the trinitarian, eternal, constant passion of love that freely chooses to create a world of creatures and to embrace these creatures in the incarnation. The particularity of the incarnation can teach us that this divine passionate love is not only general but engages with the particular and the concrete. Divine passionate love embraces each specific creature in the divine act of creation and new creation in Christ. In the light of the incarnation and the cross, it is appropriate to speak of God's compassionate suffering with suffering creation as long as compassionate suffering with creatures is affirmed of God by way of analogy; where it is understood that God's capacity for feeling with creation, springing from eternal divine passionate love, is a capacity that God possesses in a completely transcendent way, infinitely beyond human capacities for empathy with others.

Walter Kasper points out that to speak of divine suffering with creation is not the expression of a lack in God but the expression of a capacity to love in a transcendent and divine way. God does not suffer from lack of being but suffers out of love that is the overflow of the divine being.[27] Suffering does not befall God but expresses the

---

27. The Jewish theologian Abraham Heschel contrasts the biblical theology of divine pathos, expressed in the prophetic literature, with the Greek

divine freedom to love. A self-giving love involves allowing the other to affect oneself. Thus, "suffering and love go together."[28] This is not a passive being-affected but a free, active allowing the other to affect oneself. Because God is love, God can suffer with us. For Elizabeth Johnson, too, analogical speech about the suffering of God does not mean that God suffers because of some intrinsic deficiency or because of some external force. It does not mean that God suffers by necessity or that God suffers passively. It points, rather, "to an act of freedom, the freedom of love deliberately and generously shared."[29] Divine suffering with us springs from the compassionate loving act of the triune God in creating a world of creatures and embracing them in redemptive love.

Christian believers are surely right to see in the cross the symbol of a God who loves us with a love that involves a compassion, a suffering with us, beyond any human capacity for being with another in their pain. It is not that the human physical and emotional states of Jesus are simply transferred to the life of the eternal Trinity. Rather, it is that the passionate love of God-with-us expressed in the cross represents the truth of the transcendent God's capacity to be with creatures in boundless passionate love. The gospel tradition of the glorious risen Christ still bearing the wounds of the cross suggests that the sufferings of creation are forever remembered and taken up in the healing, compassionate love of God.

7. Beauty and Violence in Nature and the Work of Love

Annie Dillard's *Pilgrim at Tinker Creek* is a powerful reflection on the natural world, based on a year of living quietly at Tinker Creek, in the Roanoke Valley of Virginia, observing nature closely, backed by wide reading in the sciences and in theology.[30] Her work asks

---

philosophical concept of God's immutability; see Abraham J. Heschel, *The Prophets*, vol. 2. (New York: Harper & Row, 1962), 1–47.

28. Kasper, *God of Jesus Christ*, 196.

29. Elizabeth Johnson, *She Who Is: The Mystery of God in Feminist Theological Discourse* (New York: Crossroad, 1992), 266–67.

30. Annie Dillard, *Pilgrim at Tinker Creek* (New York: HarperPerennial, 1974, 1999).

fundamental questions: Is the natural world unutterably beautiful, so that if we took the time to really see we would be transformed? Or is it extremely wasteful and violent in a way that we seldom face? The same questions arise for many who watch the brilliantly executed television documentaries on the natural world presented by David Attenborough and others.

I am convinced that the natural world is profoundly beautiful and that its beauty has always nourished human existence, art, and spirituality. Over and over again, in ever new ways, it is experienced as absolute gift. But it is also deeply ambiguous. No one can delight in the predation, the pain, and the enormous scale of loss in nature. In our time, we know, in a way that earlier generations did not, that the costs are not extrinsic but profoundly built into evolutionary emergence and the way the natural world functions. The beautiful and the violent are in many cases two sides of the one reality. As Holmes Rolston puts it, "The cougar's fangs have carved the limbs of the fleet-footed deer, and vice versa."[31]

So can we affirm without reservation simply from observation that the natural world is unambiguously good? I think that, from empirical observation alone, this could be said only with important reservations. Biblical faith, of course, does pronounce creation as good. But as Christopher Southgate notes, in his important treatment of these issues, biblical faith actually affirms both the "good" and the "groaning" of creation.[32] Without revelation, simply on the basis of observation and reason, it is possible to come to the conclusion that there is a Creator and to believe in the goodness of the Creator. But there are also real obstacles in the way of these positions because of the ambiguity and violence in the natural world, of which we humans are a part.

For Christianity, the affirmation that creation is unambiguously the work of love is an affirmation that comes from revelation in Christ. It is affirmed on the basis of faith in the God revealed in Christ and in hope in this God's eschatological healing and fulfillment.

31. Holmes Rolston III, *Science and Religion: A Critical Survey* (1987; repr., Philadelphia and London: Templeton Foundation Press, 2006), 134.

32. Christopher Southgate, *The Groaning of Creation: God, Evolution, and the Problem of Evil* (Louisville, KY: Westminster John Knox Press, 2008), 1–18.

The nature of God is revealed in Jesus of Nazareth, in his life, death, and resurrection, as a God of radical love. On this basis, on faith, we can affirm not only the unqualified goodness of the Creator but also the unqualified goodness of creation when it is fulfilled in Christ. Meanwhile, creation is "groaning in labor pains until now; and not only the creation, but we ourselves, who have the first fruits of the Spirit, groan inwardly while we wait for adoption, the redemption of our bodies" (Rom 8:22-23). The rest of the natural world, too, needs redemption, healing, and transfiguration in Christ. What is not obvious to empirical observation can be affirmed in the light of Christ: the natural world is entirely the work of divine love, destined for fulfillment in God. It was long ago affirmed on the basis of Jewish faith by the author of the Wisdom of Solomon:

> For you love all things that exist,
> and detest none of the things that you have made,
> for you would not have made anything if you had hated it.
> How would anything have endured if you had not willed it?
> Or how would anything not called forth by you have been
>   preserved?
> You spare all things, for they are yours, O Lord, you who love
>   the living.
> For your immortal spirit is in all things (Wis 11:24–12:1).

Chapter 2

Subdue and Conquer:
An Ecological Perspective on Genesis 1:28

Antoinette Collins

If religious attitudes have helped to create the environmental crises we now face, then in order to change human behavior toward greater responsibility for global flourishing, religion needs to be part of the solution. Science and religion need to work together.[1] This essay addresses the need to transform not simply the material environment but, even more critically, to transform our human attitudes, behaviors, and politics in ways that value the full flourishing of life on earth. We need to start at the beginning of the Bible, particularly with Genesis 1:28, which will be the main focus here. The interpretation of these words has significantly influenced the attitude of

---

1. See Lynn White Jr., "The Historical Roots of Our Ecological Crisis," *Science* 155 (1967): 1203–7. Heated debate has been raging before and after the Lynn White thesis on Genesis and ecology. Genesis 1:26-28, the focus of this essay, has been part of that discussion. For a concise overview of the Lynn White follow-up debate, see John Rogerson, "The Creation Stories: Their Ecological Potential and Problems," in *Ecological Hermeneutics: Biblical, Historical and Theological Perspectives*, ed. David G. Horrell, et. al., 21–31 (London: T&T Clark International, 2010). For further dialogue on the Lynn White thesis, see also H. Paul Santmire, *Nature Reborn: The Ecological and Cosmic Promise of Christian Theology* (Minneapolis: Fortress Press, 2000), 10–15.

humanity regarding the care of the environment, hence the need for a renewed discussion of the original texts and their translations. The Bible can and should offer a theology of creation from which a new ethic can emerge to influence judgments and behaviors that favor eco-justice and environmental responsibility.

1. Subdue and Conquer

Genesis 1:28 states: "God blessed them, and God said to them, 'Be fruitful and multiply, and fill the earth and subdue [*kabash*] it; and have dominion [*radah*] over the fish of the sea and over the birds of the air and over every living thing that moves upon the earth.'" Today this text in our English translations does not reverberate harmoniously in our sensitive ecological ears. "Filling the earth" and overpopulating it sounds frighteningly unsustainable for contemporary thinking.[2] Unfortunately the Hebrew of Genesis 1:28 does not resound with melodious harmony either. "Subdue (or conquer) the earth" is rendered in Hebrew by the verb *kabash*, which can also mean "bring into bondage, dominate."[3] Moreover, in later Hebrew, for example in the book of Esther, it refers to the domination, subduing, or even raping of women: "The Hebrew verb *kabas* [*sic*] is one of several that express the exercise of force. The meaning of *kabas* can be realized in various contexts: in military hostilities, when whole territories and their populations are subdued . . . but also in individual cases when someone is enslaved, or in the sexual realm when a woman or girl . . . is assaulted."[4]

---

2. It is worth noting here that Australian Aboriginal people controlled their population for centuries before European settlement in Australia; see Bill Gammage, *The Biggest Estate on Earth: How Aborigines Made Australia* (Sydney: Allen & Unwin, 2012), 150.

3. Francis Brown, S. R. Driver, and Charles A. Briggs, eds., *A Hebrew and English Lexicon of the Old Testament* (Oxford: Clarendon Press, 1977), 461.

4. G. Johannes Botterweck, Helmer Ringgren, et al., eds. *Theological Dictionary of the Old Testament* 7 (Grand Rapids, MI: Eerdmans, 1995), 56. But note the caution of Terence Fretheim who points out that the sense of "subdue" and "co-coercion" involves *interhuman* relationships and Genesis 1:28 is the only place where the verb is used of nonhuman creation; this "means that one cannot simply transfer to this text understandings from its usage for human activities."

As Norman Habel states, "There is nothing gentle about the verb *kabash*"—subdue.[5] Furthermore, and rather poignantly, in Genesis 1:28 the word for earth, *erets*, is feminine, and so the Hebrew can be translated "fill the earth and subdue her" with the feminine pronominal suffix "her" to agree with earth. When the text is read in Hebrew, feminist critical perspectives acutely recognize the harshness of the expression. Such grammatical occurrences may or may not have had interpretive meaning when they were written then, and/or now; nonetheless many ecologists today, and not only ecofeminists, would consider that our conquering of the earth is not unlike rape and has been caused by human and/or especially male aggressive activity. It is relevant to recall here that rape is considered to be a crime of power not sexual passion; it is a crime of violence that has little to do with sexuality.[6] In fact, the environment is healthier and better survives in countries where violence against women has decreased.[7] If violence against women disappeared, ecological health would benefit. The two seem to be correlative.[8] From these findings, it could follow that if all violence vanished from our society,

---

See Terence E. Fretheim, *God and World in the Old Testament: A Relational Theology of Creation* (Nashville, TN: Abingdon Press, 2005), 52.

5. Norman Habel, "Geophany: The Earth Story in Genesis 1," in *The Earth Story in Genesis*, ed. Norman Habel (Sheffield, UK: Sheffield Academic Press, 2000), 47.

6. A. Nicholas Groth and H. Jean Birnbaum, *Men Who Rape: The Psychology of the Offender* (New York: Plenum Press, 1979), 5; cited by Pamela Cooper-White, *The Cry of Tamar: Violence against Women and the Church's Response* (Minneapolis: Fortress Press, 1995), 84–85. Groth states: "Rape is a pseudosexual act, a pattern of behavior that is concerned much more with status, hostility, control, and dominance than with sensual pleasure or sexual satisfaction. It is sexual behavior in the primary service of non-sexual needs."

7. See, for example, Vandana Shiva, "Let Us Survive: Women, Ecology and Development," in Rosemary Radford Ruether, *Women Healing Earth* (New York: Orbis Books, 1996), 70: "In the perspective of women engaged in survival struggles, which are simultaneously struggles for the protection of nature, women and nature are intimately related, and their domination and liberation similarly linked. The women's movement and the ecology movement are therefore one and are primarily counter trends to patriarchal maldevelopment."

8. "Our loss of connection with the world and with other human beings is also at the center of violence against women" (see Cooper-White, *The Cry of Tamar*, 19).

our planet would flourish ecologically and, undoubtedly, in every other way.

In a similar line of thought, the English Jesuit poet Gerard Manley Hopkins, in the mid-nineteenth century, prophetically displayed a growing awareness of the ecological problem of subduing the earth, for even though he eloquently affirms that "the world is charged with the grandeur of God," in the same poem he also laments that

> all is seared with trade; bleared, smeared with toil;
> And wears man's smudge and shares man's smell: the soil
> is bare now, nor can foot feel being shod.[9]

In the next stanza of this famous sonnet, however, Hopkins is more hopeful:

> And for all this nature is never spent;
> There lives the dearest freshness deep down things.

These words suggest the tenacity of mother/woman nature. The raped feminine earth maintains her capacity for life in the face of the searing trade and being "smeared with toil." But can we in the twenty-first century be as optimistic today as Hopkins was in the nineteenth century?

The correlation between human behavior and ecological health is also raised by John Rogerson with his insight that, prior to the flood narrative, the relationship between human and nonhuman living creatures is "one of mutual harmony."[10] He continues: "This is of importance for the understanding of the verbs *kabash* and *radah*, because whatever they may mean in other contexts, in Genesis 1 they occur in the context of a non-violent world. Any coercive sense that they possess has to be understood in a non-violent way."[11] Rogerson further supports his idea by citing P. Beauchamp: "The bible

---

9. "God's Grandeur," in *The Poems of Gerard Manley Hopkins*, ed. W. H. Gardner and N. H. MacKenzie, 4th ed. (Oxford: Oxford University Press, 1970), 66.

10. Rogerson, "The Creation Stories," 26.

11. Ibid.

does not think of peace between human beings without peace between humans and animals."[12]

Such thinking returns us to Genesis 1:28. The word in the text after *kabash* ("subdue") does not improve the situation at all; *radah* means "have dominion, rule, dominate."[13] It is often translated as *"be masters of the fish of the sea and over the birds of the air, and over every living thing crawling on the earth"* (Gen 1:28).[14] It is this attitude of ruthless dominion of the earth and her creatures that challenges us today. Can we redeem the bleak meanings/translations of these two words *kabash* ("subdue") and *radah* ("dominate") into an eco-relevant interpretation suitable to our time? Can we, like the rabbis of the Talmud and Mishnah, allow the text to continue to be a living text that equips us to practice *tikkun olam* ("the healing of the world")?[15]

2. The Greek, Aramaic, and Latin Translations

Early translations of the Hebrew text, such as the Greek, Aramaic, and Latin, offer significant insights into the interpretation of the

---

12. Ibid; here citing Paul Beauchamp, "Création et fondation de la loi en Gen, 1:1-2,4," in F. Blanquart, ed., *La Création dans l'orient ancien* (Paris: Cerf, 1987), 180.

13. Brown, Driver, and Briggs, *A Hebrew and English Lexicon of the Old Testament*, 921–22.

14. There are various translations today; nonetheless, it is still difficult to soften the meaning in English. Other translation examples include: *"rule* the fish of the sea, the birds of the sky, and all the living things that creep on the earth"* (W. G. Plaut, ed., *The Torah* [New York: Union of American Hebrew Congregations, 1981]); *"Be masters* of the fish of the sea, the birds of heaven and all living animals on the earth"* (*The Jerusalem Bible* [London: Darton, Longman and Todd, 1966]); *"Have dominion* over the fish of the sea, and over the fowl of the air, and over every living thing that moveth upon the earth"* (*Holy Bible: King James Version*, 2009 [Electronic Edition of the 1900 Authorized Version. Bellingham, WA: Logos Research Systems, Inc.]).

15. "The root *t-k-n* appears only three times in the Bible, all in Ecclesiastes (1:15, 7:13, 12:9)." Here in Ecclesiastes it is used in the sense of straighten, amend, or restore. "*Tikkun olam* is also a basic kabbalistic concept, as the Kabbalah regards the world order as shattered, to be restored to its earlier perfection only through *tikkun olam.*" *The New Encyclopedia of Judaism*, s.v. "Tikkum Olam," accessed May 3, 2012, http://www.credoreference.com/entry/nyupencyjud/tikkun_olam.

Hebrew terms *kabash* and *radah*. How do these ancient interpreters deal with such harsh vocabulary? These three representative translation traditions will be considered here as a sample of the variations that can occur in other languages and thus early interpretations of Genesis 1:28.

The Greek Septuagint

The Septuagint of Genesis 1:28 translates *kabash* ("subdue") as *katakyrieusate* and *radah* ("dominate") as *archete*. *Katakyrieō* can mean: "1. To gain dominion over; 2. To exercise absolute authority over."[16] *Katakyrieō* could also be interpreted to mean like a lord (*kyrios*) or indeed like "the Lord." In fact, in Jeremiah 3:14 it refers to the "benign government of God":[17] "Come back disloyal children—it is the Lord [*Kyrios*] who speaks— for I alone am your master [*katakyrieuso*]. I will take one from a town, two from a clan, and bring you to Zion. I will give you shepherds after my own heart and these shall feed you on knowledge and discretion" (Jer 3:14; author's translation). A very gentle, pastoral "mastering" on God's part is expressed here by the word *katakyrieo*.

The Greek *archete*, used to translate the Hebrew *radah* in Genesis 1:28 (have dominion over), means to regulate (see Gen 1:18) or to rule over and does not have the same violent tone of the Hebrew.[18] Rulers can be benign or tyrannical, but at least with the use of this Greek word, there exists the possibility of a less destructively powerful reign. Indeed, in a temporal sense, *archai* can also mean "to make a

---

16. Takamitsu Muraoka, *A Greek-English Lexicon of the Septuagint* (Louvain: Peeters, 2009), 374.

17. Henry G. Liddell and Robert Scott, eds., *An Intermediate Greek-English Lexicon* (Oxford: Clarendon Press, 1896), 409. Interestingly, the Hebrew of Jeremiah 3:14 has *Baaliti*; literally translated this can mean "I will marry [you]," which suggests someone as benign as a loving husband! Biblical examples of a benign and loving husband in the scriptural world of patriarchy may seem difficult to find, but they do exist; some instances could include: Jacob and Rachel in Genesis; Elkanah and Hannah in 1 Samuel 1; Hosea is certainly encouraged to act in this way with God as a model in the book of Hosea; and Joseph toward Mary in Matthew's infancy narratives (Matt 1 and 2).

18. Muraoka, *A Greek-English Lexicon of the Septuagint*, 95–96.

beginning."[19] Once again, the Greek translation presents a more moderate interpretation.

The Aramaic Targums

The Aramaic Targums or Targumim are always helpful as they provide not just a translation but an interpretation as well. The paraphrastic nature of the Targumim offers more detailed insights into the thinking of the community behind the text. Whereas the Greek and the Latin strive to be more literal and accurate, the Targumim reflect the thinking at their time of composition—100 BCE to 200 CE. There are three major Targumic traditions: Targum Onkelos, Targum Neofiti, and Targum Pseudo Jonathan, which is otherwise known as the Jerusalem Targum or the Targum of the Land of Israel due to its Palestinian provenance; however, we will consider mainly Targum Pseudo Jonathan in this sample, as it is generally the most interpretive and creative of the Targums.[20] This particular translation has for the Hebrew *kabash* the verb *takaph*—"to seize, to overpower"[21]—which does not sound particularly temperate. The noun *tekoph*, based on the verb *takaph*, means, however, "strength, power, help, protection"[22] and so has an impression of "care." For *radah*, Targum Pseudo Jonathan has *shalat*, "to handle, to rule, to

---

19. Henry Liddell, *An Intermediate Greek-English Lexicon Founded upon the Seventh Edition of Liddell and Scott's Greek-English Lexicon* (Oak Harbor, WA: Logos Research Systems, 1996).

20. Dating the Targums is difficult, but the discovery of Targums at Qumran proves the antiquity of transliterating the Hebrew text into Aramaic; some elements of Pseudo Jonathan may go back to 100 BCE. See the discussion by Gerard J. Norton, "Ancient Versions and Textual Transmission of the Old Testament," in *The Oxford Handbook of Biblical Studies*, http://www.oxfordbiblicalstudies.com .ezproxy2.acu.edu.au/article/book/obso-9780199254255/obso-9780199254255 -div1-75?_hi=3&_pos=3#match (accessed March 5, 2012).

Other scholars consider *Ps-Jon* quite late, possibly as late as the seventh/ eighth century CE, but there is evidence that earlier strata predated the Mishnah; see Philip S. Alexander, "Targum, Targumim," in *The Anchor Yale Bible Dictionary*, vol. 6, ed. David N. Freedman (New York: Doubleday, 1996), 321.

21. Marcus Jastrow, *A Dictionary of the Targumim, the Talmud Babli and Yerushalmi, and the Midrashic Literature* (New York: Judaica Press Inc., 1975), 1693.

22. Ibid., 1690.

have power over,"[23] suggesting a more benign "ruling." Moreover, the Palestinian Talmud (PT) also uses *shalat* in the sense of power of attorney over another's property.[24] Again, a gentler interpretation all around. So there is a developing and/or softening of the Hebrew. It would be appropriate here to quote two examples of the Targums by way of comparison for their translation/interpretation of Genesis 1:28. They are similar to Genesis and to each other, but their Aramaic vocabulary as indicated above is different.

> And the Lord blessed them, and said to them, "Spread abroad, and become many, and fill the earth, and be strong upon it; and have dominion over the fish of the sea, and over the fowl of the heavens, and over every living thing that moveth upon the earth." (Targum Onkelos Gen 1:28)[25]

> God blessed them, and God said to them, "Increase and multiply and fill the earth with sons and daughters, and become powerful in possessions upon it, and have dominion over the fish of the sea and over the birds of the heavens, and over every creeping animal that creeps upon the earth." (Targum Pseudo Jonathan Gen 1:28)[26]

The Latin Vulgate

The Latin of the Vulgate will be our final textual comparison. For *kabash* ("subdue") it uses *subiicite*, while for *radah* ("have dominion, rule, and dominate") it uses *dominamini*. *Subiicite* is the Latin word of choice for *radah* and would seem to be related to the root *subicio* rather than the similar *subigo*. The latter of these two words can have the more severe meaning of "subjugation," but the translators/editors of the Vulgate have not chosen it. *Subiicite* can be translated as "to throw under, place under, set up, make subject, submit, ascribe."[27]

23. Ibid., 1581.

24. Ibid., 1581 and 1690.

25. *The Targum Onqelos to Genesis* (Wilmington, DE: Michael Glazier, 1988).

26. Michael Maher, *Targum Pseudo Jonathan: Genesis. Translated with Introduction and Notes*, The Aramaic Bible Volume 1b (Collegeville, MN: Liturgical Press, 1987).

27. See Charlton T. Lewis and Charles Short, *A Latin Dictionary* (Oxford: Clarendon Press, 1922), 1776–77.

The other word under consideration—*radah*—is rendered in the Latin by *dominamini*, meaning "to be Lord, to reign, to govern, to rule, to command."[28] *Dominamini* could suggest Godlikeness (*Dominus*—"the Lord") as verse 26 maintains: "Then God said: 'Let us make humankind in our image, . . . in the image of God he created them; male and female he created them" (Gen 1:26). Made in God's image, we must therefore be Godlike. Here is a similar interpretation to the Greek with its use of *Katakyrieō, Kyrios* ("Lord") and *archete, arkon* ("ruler").[29]

The following table summarizes the linguistic comparison discussed above:

HEBREW Masoretic	GREEK Septuagint	ARAMAIC Targum	LATIN Vulgate
KABASH "Subdue"	*Katakurieusate* "Power, lordship over." Benign/pastoral power of God (Jer 3:14)	*takaph*— "to seize, to overpower." The noun *tikooph* based on the verb means "strength, power, help, protection."	*Subiicite*—to throw under, place under, set up, make subject, submit, ascribe
RADAH "Have dominion"	*Archete* "Rule" *archai* (beginning, a founding leader)	*Shalat* "To handle, rule, to have power over" P.T. uses *shalat* in the sense of "power of attorney over another's property"	*Dominamini* "to be Lord, to reign, to govern, to rule, to command"— in a godly way.

3. Contextual Interpretation of Genesis 1:28

> Then God said, "Let us make humankind in our image, according to our likeness; and let them have dominion over

28. Ibid., 608–9.
29. See further perspectives on this interpretation following in this essay.

[*veyiredu*] the fish of the sea, and over the birds of the air, and over the cattle, and over all the wild animals of the earth, and over every creeping thing that creeps upon the earth." So God created humankind in his image, in the image of God he created them; male and female he created them. God blessed them, and God said to them, "Be fruitful and multiply, and fill the earth and subdue it [*vekiveshuah*]; and have dominion [*uredu*] over the fish of the sea and over the birds of the air and over every living thing that moves upon the earth." (Gen 1:26-28)

A closer look at the Genesis text above, even in the English translation, intimately associates humankind with "the image" and "likeness" of God. This humanity, made in God's image is then blessed with the ability to be cocreators of life, "be fruitful," and in this context is told to "subdue" (*kiveshuah*) and "have dominion over" (*uredu*) the earth. Thus being made in God's image and recipients of God's blessing qualifies the intention of "to subdue" and "to have dominion" over. It follows that human domination is an authority conferred by God, a sharing in God's governance that must continue God's creative goodness. Human rule, in this context, is intended to have a constructive outcome, as Claus Westermann states: "In ruling, humans must preserve humanity and remain humane."[30] Therefore, human dominion can be interpreted as a responsibility for which humans are answerable to God and the whole of creation. Human dominion over the earth should therefore embrace the conservation and flourishing of God's creation.[31]

4. The Earth-Centered Story in Genesis 1

Along a similar continuum but from a slightly differing perspective Norman Habel argues that the creation story of Genesis 1 is primarily about *ha erets*—the earth—and that the short, five-verse human story in Genesis 1:26-30 contravenes the spirit of the twenty-

30. Claus Westermann cited in H-J. Zobel, *"Rada," Theological Dictionary of the Old Testament*, vol. 3, ed. G. J. Botterweck, et al. (Grand Rapids, MI: Eerdmans, 2004), 335.

31. Ibid., 335–36.

five-verse Earth-oriented story that precedes it in Genesis 1:1-25. As Habel argues, an anthropocentric interpretation of Genesis 1 demotes the Earth story to an obviously inferior position. The much shorter story of the creation of humankind has superseded the much longer story of cosmic creation.[32] Habel persuasively maintains that "the story of humans subduing Earth has suppressed the story of a pristine Earth of intrinsic worth."[33] Indeed, Habel formulates the valid point that "no reason is given as to why a pristine Earth . . . should need to be subdued" or controlled. In fact, *Elohim* finds Earth good in all her aspects. We can move on from a totally anthropocentric view of creation to one that is more relational and reverential. Such a view is found among many cultures prior to the "civilizing" influence of Western colonization; Aboriginal Australia will provide one such example.

5. Australian Aboriginal Ecology

Eugene Stockton reported that Aboriginal people "in the harshest inhabited continent on earth"[34] survived by caring for the land and by turning that survival into a lifestyle and indeed a spirituality.[35] As early as 1953, William Stanner described the Aboriginal people thus: "They neither dominate their environment nor seek to change it. . . . One can only say they are 'at one' with nature. The whole ecological principle of their life might be summed up in the Baconian aphorism—*natura non vincitur nisi parendo*—'nature is not to be conquered except by obeying.' "[36]

---

32. Habel, "Geophany: The Earth Story in Genesis 1," 47. This view is supported by the fact that scientists now reckon the cosmos to be approximately 13.6 billion years old, while our own species is considered to be only 3.4 million years.

33. Ibid.

34. Eugene Stockton, *The Aboriginal Gift* (Alexandria, VA: Millennium Books, 1995), 18.

35. Ibid.

36. See Stockton, *The Aboriginal Gift*, 25. It is important to note also that the extinction of certain species and the appearance of early humans in Australia seem correlative. Josephine Flood notes, "Directly or indirectly Aboriginal occupation of the continent had as great an impact on Australian fauna in the

Stanner further describes their utilization of the land, even mining of the land,[37] but it is a different use of the land from that of
Europeans.

> The activities, at least in the short term did little to change
> the landscape except that the burning of grass to flush game
> produced bushfires that often ran for long distances. The
> vegetation suffered severely and, in consequence, plants and
> animal populations must have changed radically over millen-
> nia of occupations, enforcing new human adaptations, but
> there can have been few countries where more than 1000
> generations left so few physical traces.[38]

Furthermore, the early European settlers did not understand the
devastation they were inflicting on the land and the resultant destruction of the food supply for the local Aboriginal population: "The first
colonists had no comprehension that Sydney Cove had vital importance for a whole band (clan/mob) which was necessarily driven to
depend on other places for food and water, to the embarrassment of
other groups."[39]

Bill Gammage in his recent, controversial, yet thoroughly re-
searched work, *The Biggest Estate on Earth: How Aborigines Made Australia*, claims that the Aboriginal people of Australia, prior to white
colonization, used land management techniques employing prudent
and judicious use of fire. In doing so, they created woodlands and
grassy plains maintained in perfect ecological balance.[40] Gammage
states that three rules of land management existed prior to and in
1788:

Pleistocene as European settlement was to have in recent times." See Josephine
Flood, *Archaeology of the Dreamtime: The Story of Prehistoric Australia and Its People*
(Pymble: Angus and Robertson, 1992), 158 and 157–70.

37. William E. H. Stanner, *The Dreaming and Other Essays* (Melbourne: Black
Ink Agenda, 2009), 84.

38. Ibid.

39. Ibid., 101–2

40. See Bill Gammage, *The Biggest Estate on Earth—How Aborigines Made
Australia* (Sydney: Allen & Unwin, 2011), e.g., 6, 8–17.

1. Ensure that all life flourishes.
2. Make plants and animals abundant, convenient, and predictable.
3. Think universal, act local.[41]

We have much to learn in Australia, if it is not too late, and the knowledge of land management learned over centuries may already be lost. Gammage sadly states: "Knowledge of how to sustain Australia, of how to be Australian, vanished with barely a whisper of regret. We have a continent to learn. If we are to survive, let alone feel at home, we must begin to understand our country. If we succeed, one day we might become Australian."[42]

Conclusion

We need to "ensure that all life flourishes"[43] in our country and on our planet. The words of Genesis 1:28, "subdue and conquer"—*kabash* and *radah*—have supported for centuries the searing misuse and irresponsible exploitation of our planet. The discussion of these biblical words, located in their textual context of "blessing" (Gen 1:28) and "image and likeness" (Gen 1:26) of God, brings a different understanding into play. A newer mind-set of earth management as well as biblical interpretation is needed and possible. Creation maintenance is expected to be undertaken as a share in the God-like activity of responsible care. The Greek, Aramaic, and Latin translations of Genesis 1:28 indicate a moderation in meaning and perception of the harsher-sounding original Hebrew language—a moderation often lost not only in translations but also in practice. The necessity to shift from an anthropocentric perspective to planetary awareness is to be encouraged. The Australian Aboriginal people provide an important model of earth management learned through the wisdom of centuries of lived interaction with the flora and fauna of the land. Their living relationship with land became a lifestyle and spirituality—indeed *covenant* is not too strong a concept to describe their

41. Ibid., 4.
42. Ibid., 323.
43. Ibid., 4.

intimacy with land. Their intimacy with the land made Australia livable, flourishing, and sustainable for them. Humanity urgently needs to heed and apply their ways of planetary living. Hopkins's gentleness toward the feminine "her" challenges us today, inviting us into the biblical view where the earth, *ha adamah*, is feminine in form, and from this mother-earth, the creature *Adam* emerges (Gen 2:7). The beauty and vulnerability of earth is evoked in Hopkins's lament:

> O if we but knew what we do
> When we delve or hew—
> Hack and rack the growing green!
> Since country is so tender
> To touch, her being so slender,
> That, like this sleek and seeing ball
> But a prick will make no eye at all.[44]

44. "Binsey Poplars," in Gardner and MacKenzie, *The Poems of Gerard Manley Hopkins*, 78.

Chapter 3

If Not Now, When?
The Ecological Potential of Isaiah's
"New Things"

Dermot Nestor

"Literature is news that stays news."
Ezra Pound, *ABC of Reading*[1]

Appearing both early and emphatically within what has recently been described as one of the most provocative works of literary criticism to emerge in the twentieth century,[2] Pound's summons to embrace the literary classics of the past contains an almost prophetic tone when read against the more sterile aspects of our postmodern world. Courting the would-be writer to indulge his own intellectual yearning for a "return to origins," Pound sought tirelessly to promote an appreciation of the transformative power of past literature, works which, to his mind, not only broke fresh ground or revealed new formal techniques but possess a sort of energy, "a force transfusing, welding and unifying."[3] While Pound's select pantheon of such "axes of reference" is one which openly courts revision and challenge, his

---

1. Ezra Pound, *ABC of Reading*, with an introduction by Michael Dirda (New York: New Directions, 2010), 27.
2. Ibid., 2.
3. Ibid., 7.

adrenalized conviction that it is *only* those works of "first intensity" whose luminous details can deepen both our understanding and our lives could be seen to underpin the entire project of recovering a biblically based environmentalism.

1. Stating the Issue

The basis for this project is undoubtedly Lynn White Jr.'s seminal article published in 1967.[4] Writing as both a medieval historian and a churchman, White's charge was, in essence, that a Christian anthropocentric view of the natural world was responsible for the modern ecological crisis. The burden of guilt he placed squarely at the door of the Genesis creation accounts and particularly the conception of man and woman, uniquely created in God's image, who are granted "dominion over" (*radah*) and charged with "subduing" (*kabash*) the earth. It is this dualism between an effectively redundant nature and a dynamic, vigorous humanity that not only validates the exploitation of the former but also enshrines any implied indifference to the natural realm as "God's will." Thus, while the march of technological progress, which has so characterized Western Christendom, has certainly contributed to a perception of the West as the engine of progress,[5] it is, for White, a progress to be understood squarely within the context of the Christian dogma of humanity's transcendence of, and rightful mastery over, nature; herein, according to White, lies the biblical roots of our current ecological crisis.

Although White's charge against Judeo-Christian theology is not an isolated one,[6] it is certainly the most cited and, as such, the one around which much current debate has tended to revolve. As David Horrell and others have remarked, however, such debate is a multi-

4. Lynn White Jr., "The Historical Roots of Our Ecological Crisis," *Science* 155 (1967): 1203–7.
5. For a slightly more right-wing interpretation of this thesis, see Niall Ferguson, *Civilization: The West and the Rest* (New York: Penguin Press, 2011).
6. See H. Paul Santmire, *The Travail of Nature: The Ambiguous Ecological Promise of Christian Theology* (Philadelphia: Fortress Press, 1985), and Carl Amery, *Das Ende der Vorsehung. Die gnadenlosen Folgen des Christentums* (Reinbek: Rowohlt, 1972).

faceted and at times curious-headed monster.[7] At the more populous end of the spectrum are those who seek to transcend, if not negate, White's contention that the Bible promotes, in fact, endorses, an aggressive exploitation of nature. Their goal is to retrieve specific texts, such as Genesis 1:28, as the basis for a biblical and theologically accountable environmental ethic, one geared very much toward a care of the natural environment. Such efforts, however, find their virtual antithesis within certain evangelical traditions where a sense of "presentism" with respect to an impending apocalypse tends to condition adherents to abandon environmentalism as either a misconceived priority or a satanic new age deception.[8] Rather than invoking a sense of engagement with the potential inevitability of environmental annihilation, they sound a retreat, convinced that any alternative action is merely an obstacle to a divinely appointed end.

In many ways, such diversity of interpretation serves to point up what Francesca Stavrakopolou has recently identified as the twin axes of *accountability* and *authority*, which define most ecological engagement with biblical material.[9] On the one hand, the divinely ordained centrality of humanity *authorizes* either the demotion of the created order to secondary status, or in its most extreme form, a total abandonment of any concern with the woes of that realm. Such *authorization* is read in the opposite direction by those who seek to highlight within the biblical texts the imperative of *accountability* for the created order. Once subjected to a critical and self-conscious hermeneutical strategy, the Bible, it is argued, can reveal its "green" ecological vision.[10] Despite the polarized agendas such interpretative strategies pursue, they are united by the far more pertinent, if not

7. David G. Horrell, Cherryl Hunt, and Christopher Southgate, "Appeals to the Bible in Ecotheology and Environmental Ethics: A Typology of Hermeneutical Approaches," *SCE* 21 (2008): 219–38.

8. See Harry O. Maier, "Green Millennialism: American Evangelicals, Environmentalism and the Book of Revelation," in *Ecological Hermeneutics: Biblical, Historical and Theological Perspectives*, ed. David G. Horrell, Cherryl Hunt, Christopher Southgate, and Francesca Stavrakopolou (London/New York: T&T Clark International, 2010), 246–66.

9. Francesca Stavrakopolou, "Introduction to Part 1," in *Ecological Hermeneutics*, 15.

10. *The Green Bible* (New York: HarperOne, 2008).

logically prior, question—that of *appropriateness*. How appropriate is it to appeal to the biblical literature for the purposes of generating a response, positive or negative, to the crisis identified by White? Is the Bible really an eco-aware resource?

2. How Can an Ancient Text Address Modern Issues?

In seeking to recruit the Bible for an ecological cause, one is faced immediately with the problem of its essential "otherness." Virtually every line of its sometimes tortured prose, its enigmatic poetics, and its occasionally uncomfortable legal formulations is about people of another time and another place, people who spoke a different language and whose social and cultural norms are at a significant remove to our own. So accustomed have we become to this fact that it is worth pausing to call attention to the obvious. Since Ibn Ezra's original disputation of Mosaic authorship of the Pentateuch in the Middle Ages, the entire history of critical biblical scholarship has been punctuated by a series of epiphanies which, collectively, have served to accentuate the distance, be it chronological, cultural, or cognitive, which separates the world of the Bible from contemporary society.[11] Despite any assumed familiarity with the world of ancient Israel that may result from our own biblical heritage, the traditions of the Hebrew Bible with their "still burning passions . . . their anger, dreams [and] allusions"[12] constitute a complexity which every interpretive agenda must engage rather than simply ignore. While not quite the "foreign country" caricatured by David Lowenthal,[13] the "past" of the biblical text records a vision whose primary and initial focus is definitely not the fractured, multicultural realm of postmodernity.

Yet while acceptance of the essential "otherness" of the various worldviews revealed within the text remains a virtual *sine qua non* for

11. For an illustration, see most recently Megan Bishop Moore and Brad E. Kelle, *Biblical History and Israel's Past: The Changing Study of the Bible and History* (Grand Rapids, MI: Eerdmans, 2011).

12. Fernand Braudel, *The Mediterranean and the Mediterranean World in the Age of Phillip II*, vol. 1 (Berkeley: University of California Press, 1996), 21.

13. David Lowenthal, *The Past Is a Foreign Country* (Cambridge, UK: Cambridge University Press, 1985). Quoted in Philip J. King and Lawrence E. Stager, *Life in Biblical Israel* (London: Westminster John Knox Press, 2001), 4.

every student of the discipline, it does *not* at the same time present an insurmountable barrier to modern, "green"-oriented agendas. [14]

On the one hand, sensitivity to this "distance" may well serve to neutralize some of the more aggressive and destructive appeals to a divinely appointed anthropocentrism, something that can surely only be applauded. At the same time, its simultaneous caution against an all too ready willingness to collapse the world of contemporary human experience into the biblical text serves to highlight the fact that a biblically based environmental ethic cannot be based upon a simplistic and/or selective reading. On the contrary, if the agenda of recovery[15] is to realize its goal, it must resist what Louis Pasteur once defined as that malfunction of the spirit which conditions us to believe things simply because we want them to be true. In mining the corpus of biblical literature, in an attempt to retrieve a persuasive biblical basis on which to construct an environmental ethic, one that addresses modern Western concerns about our role and place within creation, we need to overcome any temptation to place upon that literature an interpretative burden, which it simply cannot bear. If it is to confront and perhaps transcend the environmental threats and injustices that afflict us, a biblically based ecotheology must engineer a creative and multivalent hermeneutic which aims to fuse an attentiveness to the broad horizons of present need, with a historically informed exegesis, of both text and interpretative tradition;[16] this entails a hermeneutic which must be understood as an ongoing, rather than a definitive, attempt to discern the wood from the trees.

Such a nuanced perspective is one that informs a recently published collection of essays emanating from the collaborative research project at the University of Exeter on "Uses of the Bible in Environmental

14. On the issue of "worldviews" within the biblical tradition as they relate to environmental issues, see Hilary Marlow, *Biblical Prophets and Contemporary Environmental Ethics: Re-reading Amos, Hosea and First Isaiah* (Oxford: Oxford University Press, 2009), 95–101.

15. David G. Horrell, *The Bible and the Environment: Towards a Critical Biblical Ecological Theology* (London: Equinox, 2010), 11–20, 13.

16. Ernst M. Conradie, "The Road Towards an Ecological Biblical and Theological Hermeneutics," *Scriptura* 93 (2006): 305–14. Idem. "What on Earth Is an Ecological Hermeneutics? Some Broad Parameters," in *Ecological Hermeneutics*, 295–315.

Ethics."[17] Of particular relevance to this present study is the essay by
John Barton, which fully engages the specific issue of "appropriateness" with respect to the ecopotential of the biblical prophets.[18] Tem-
pered by a recognition of the essential "otherness" of the prophetic
worldview, any sense that Barton's essay is a simple exercise in recovery quickly evaporates. For while he is quick to identify among the
"words of the prophets most scholars consider authentic"[19] a sense of
appreciation for, if not wonder at, the "orderliness of creation when
uninterfered with by human beings,"[20] there is, he cautions, very little
else of a contemporary environmental flavor to be found within the
same sources. Issues of sustainability and pollution, of species extinction and melting ice caps were both unknown and, in many ways,
irrelevant to those who sought to stem the tide of corruption and
greed which they identified with the increased urbanization and in-
ternationalization of Israel's political and social elite. While certain
details of the prophetic critique may well resonate with specific aspects
of an environmentally oriented agenda,[21] to assume that the message
of the prophets is framed by an ecological wisdom fully conversant
with today's ills is at best apologetic and at worst anachronistic. Given
the admonitory note articulated by Barton then, any analysis of 2 Isaiah
is obliged to tread cautiously in search of its ecological credentials
rather than simply assume that they exist. It is to this task that our
attention must now turn.

3. Isaiah 40–55

Whether read as part of the larger Isaian corpus or in isolation
as a work attributed to the anonymous author, conventionally labeled

17. Horrell, et al, *Ecological Hermeneutics*.
18. John Barton, "Reading the Prophets from an Environmental Perspective,"
in *Ecological Hermeneutics*, 46–56.
19. Ibid., 47.
20. Ibid., 46.
21. Barton does recognize the potential of the story of Naboth's vineyard
recounted in 1 Kings 21 as providing a biblical basis for contemporary challenges
to what he terms "land-grabbing" (ibid., 48).

2 or Deutero-Isaiah,[22] the fifteen chapters that comprise Isaiah 40–55 offer a rich and varied portrayal of the renewal and restoration to which God is leading Israel. Almost universally accepted as emanating from the sixth-century BCE, 2 Isaiah is an intensely poetic work whose entire theology is guided by the foundational claim that YHWH is the incomparable creator God (40:18-26; 45:18-19). While there is little need to expound in detail the rhetorical landscape presumed within the work itself, or the view that the theology of 2 Isaiah is intensely "monotheistic" in its orientation,[23] it is pertinent to examine some of the bases upon which this critical claim for the singularity of God is leveraged.

In stark contrast to the judgments pronounced by 1 Isaiah (5:8-21; 8:1-22; 28:1-3), the voice behind 2 Isaiah offers no condemnation of Israel but rather a message of confident hope that the experience of "exile" will soon come to an end.

> Comfort, O comfort my people, says your God.
> Speak to the heart of Jerusalem,
> and cry to her
> that she has served her term,
> that her penalty is paid,
> that she has received from the Lord's hand
> double for all her sins. (Isa 40:1-2)[24]

22. On the various terminologies used to name and describe chapters 40–55 of Isaiah, see Ebenezer Henderson, *The Book of the Prophet Isaiah* (London: Hamilton Adams & Co., 1840); Samuel R. Driver, *An Introduction to the Literature of the Old Testament*, 9th ed. (Edinburgh: T&T Clark, 1913), 230–46; Christopher R. North, *The Second Isaiah: Introduction, Translation and Commentary to Chapters XL–LV* (Oxford: Clarendon Press, 1964), 1–30.

23. See, for example, Morton S. Smith, *The Origins of Biblical Monotheism: Israel's Polytheistic Background and the Ugaritic Texts* (Oxford: Oxford University Press, 2001), 179–95; Klaus Koch, "Ugaritic Polytheism and Hebrew Monotheism in Isaiah 40–55," in Robert P. Gordon, ed., *The God of Israel*, University of Cambridge Oriental Publications 64 (Cambridge, UK: Cambridge University Press, 2007), 205–28; Casper J. Labuschagne, *The Incomparability of Yahweh in the Old Testament*, Pretoria Oriental Series 5 (Leiden: Brill, 1966).

24. Unless otherwise stated, all translations from the Hebrew are the author's own.

Despite the richness of imagination and rhetoric that characterizes these fifteen chapters, the primary story line and core claim is simple: it is YHWH who has defeated the powers of Babylon, and it is YHWH who permits the joyous and triumphant journey home. Given the trauma of deportation that had already ensued, along with the seemingly enduring potency of their captors, it is reasonable to assume that any prophetic announcement that heralded a radical reversion of present circumstance would be met with the obduracy and intransigence that had long characterized Israel's relationship with its God. Quite simply, how could a God, whose apparent limitations had been so ruthlessly exposed, be capable of bringing to fruition such a master plan? It is this question to which the "Book of Consolation" responds.

Presenting himself in the guise of a defense counsel, the prophet immediately sets about the task of establishing YHWH's credentials in respect of any impending salvific action. While the series of rhetorical questions that frame this quasi-legal form of disputation are certainly designed to affirm that, as creator, YHWH needs no guidance, no counsel, and no teaching (40:13-14), they are anchored by a biting and satirical polemic against idol worship, which has few parallels in the Old Testament.[25] Structured so as to emphasize at every point the distance between a transcendent creator and a dependent creation, 2 Isaiah takes great pleasure in exposing the futility of both idol fabrication and idol veneration, a point made with devastating effect in 44:9-20. Here, the carpenter is caricatured as a clown who, in cleaving a tree in half, burns one portion to warm himself while simultaneously praying to the other half for his salvation:

> "He [The Carpenter] cuts down cedars or chooses a holm tree or an oak and lets it grow strong among the trees of the forest. He plants a cedar and the rain nourishes it. . . . Half of it he burns in the fire; over this half he roasts meat, eats it and is satisfied. He also warms himself and says, 'Ah, I am warm, I can feel the fire!' The rest of it he makes into a god, his idol, bows down to it and worships it; he prays to it and says, 'Save me, for you are my god!'" (Isa 44:14, 16-17; NRSV)

25. For a similar presentation of idols and idol worship, see Psalm 115:4-8 and Jeremiah 10:1-16.

Although the desired effect of mocking, deriding, and ultimately dismissing other gods as abominations who enslave their deluded devotees makes YHWH conspicuous by contrast, the success of such a strategy is based wholly on the fact that YHWH is excluded in principle from the critique.[26] Analogous to the challenge issued by Ludwig Feuerbach, and later by Sigmund Freud, that religion is nothing other than a mere "human projection,"[27] the prophet's exposure of the illusory character of idol worship is counterposed simply by the repeated affirmation that YHWH is *not* like the other gods; YHWH is the exception who demands allegiance.

The ostensible effect of insisting that YHWH is incomparable, the first and the last (44:6) besides whom there are no others (44:8), is not so much to denude Babylonian confidence as it is to empower Israel to think, to trust, and, most emphatically, to remember. While the current political marginalization and social inferiority of Israel would appear to render such a tactic somewhat naïve, it quickly becomes apparent that the prophet is pursuing an altogether different strategy. For in shifting proof of divinity away from the traditional realm of military prowess, the prophet asserts that it is the dependable and unremitting continuity between what a god *says* and what a god *does* that is the sole demonstration of his status. For 2 Isaiah, then, it is the proven ability to predict and to bring about events in the historical sphere that is the determining criterion in evaluating "divine" credentials. This sleight of hand is employed to devastating effect. The predictable silence it elicits from the Babylonian pantheon (41:28; 41:24) provides the perfect foil for the vindication of YHWH as sovereign in history and, as such, the one who *alone* is capable of predicting and ultimately setting in motion the decisive turns in history; this sovereignty is merely exemplified in the election of Cyrus (41:25).

While the prophet's attempt to establish the trustworthiness of the "new things" (43:18) announced by YHWH encompasses an

---

26. Walter Brueggemann, *Isaiah 40–55* (Louisville, KY: Westminster John Knox Press, 1998), 69.

27. Ludwig Feuerbach, *The Essence of Christianity*, trans. George Elliot (New York: Cosimo Classics, 2008). See also Hans Küng, *Does God Exist? Answer for Today*, trans. Edward Quinn (New York: Vintage Books, 1981).

appeal to the fidelity of the prophetic tradition as a whole (41:22; 42:9; 43:9; 46:9),[28] it is an argument which converges upon the Exodus event as the paradigmatic example of God's predictive and redemptive power (43:16-18). Conjured up in a series of familiar phrases and motifs such as the "passage through the mighty waters" (Exod 15:10) and the demise of both horse and chariot (Exod 15:1), the essentially analogical argument forwarded by 2 Isaiah functions to provide a climatic dismantling of the supremacy of imperial Babylon and an indisputable case for the imminent reversal of Israel's exilic status. As creator, sovereign, and declarer, it is YHWH alone who can bring and always has brought about Israel's restoration.

Although it is certainly true that the final exhortation to leave Babylon (48:20-22) does not "exhaust the scope of the authors expectations nor oblige us to domicile the author among the Jewish ethnic minority in Babylon,"[29] it is within the context of an anticipated resolution of the crisis of exile that the creation theology so long recognized as a distinctive feature of this work comes to full bloom.[30]

4. Creation in 2 Isaiah

As a theological concept, or a cultural historical perspective,[31] creation in 2 Isaiah is reducible to neither a single definitive statement nor a solitary unambiguous definition.[32] Dispersed throughout each of its carefully crafted stanzas and pervading the majority of its historically bound pronouncements, creation is something that transcends the primordial and exclusive perspective of Genesis, to imprint its grandeur across space and time. While such amorphous qualities may, at first glance, render intractable any attempt at inter-

---

28. For an alternative explanation of the significance of "former things" and "new things" in 2 Isaiah, see Brevard Childs, *Introduction to the Old Testament as Scripture* (Philadelphia: Fortress Press, 1979), 311–39.

29. Joseph Blenkinsopp, *Isaiah 40–55*, Anchor Bible 19a (New York: Doubleday, 2002), 228.

30. See, for example, North, *The Second Isaiah*.

31. See Simon Schama, *Landscape and Memory* (London: Fontana Press, 1996).

32. William P. Brown, *The Seven Pillars of Creation: The Bible, Science, and the Ecology of Wonder* (Oxford: Oxford University Press, 2010), 198.

pretation, it is this very splendor, which at every point seeks to confirm the continuity between the enduring character of creation and the redemptive power of YHWH, that furnishes a key to the author's intentions. Building upon specific themes and pronouncements of chapters 1–39, specifically those which engage the concept of "environmental transformation," the message of 2 Isaiah seems to invert the images of environmental degradation which underscore his predecessor's message of imminent and inevitable destruction (6:11; 32:13-20).

Where previously the land was depicted as reverting to its undomesticated, natural state in the wake of exile (5:17; 17:2; 27:10), in 2 Isaiah the prophet announces not just a process of reforestation (41:19) and a return to fertility (41:18) but rather a regeneration (41:17), one entirely consistent with the invitation to Israel to grow into a new community (51:3; 55:6-8).

Although the absence of any specific mention of Israel at this juncture has led some commentators to question the consensus view that the benevolent acts recounted in 41:17-20 have as their focus the returning Exiles,[33] the eagerly anticipated declaration that opens the work (40:3-5) leaves little doubt that what is being envisioned is a homecoming. For while the highway being constructed across the Arabian desert is one more befitting traffic of the divine rather than human variety,[34] the envisioned regeneration of Judah is truly in keeping with the glory of YHWH (40:5). The land previously laid waste by the Babylonian incursion (1:7) is now to be reborn (41:18-20) and in a very public manner fashioned so that "all flesh" can bear witness (40:5). While this anticipated "return" of YHWH may well be indicative of a decisive break with the idea of a territorial and locative deity, a notion also testified to in Ezekiel (9:3; 10:4; 11:22-23), it is the triumphant return of YHWH, not Israel, that is to be read as the occasion for the miraculous acts recounted in 41:17-20. The opening up of pools, rivers, and springs on the hills, plains, and deserts, along with the replanting of several species of large trees,

---

33. Joseph Blenkinsopp, *Isaiah 40–55*, 203.

34. "There is no mention here of preparing a route for return from exile in Babylon. It is, rather, that a processional way is to be prepared for the return of Yahweh to his people" (ibid., 181).

is concerned almost exclusively with the enhancement and communication of YHWH's prestige; so that

> all may see and know,
> all may consider and understand
> that the hand of YHWH has done this,
> the Holy One of Israel has created this. (41:20)

The miracle of such abundant flourishing is the decisive evidence that points to the sovereign power of YHWH: how could those looking on not believe that from this same creative hand a new future is possible?

This ability of YHWH to control and direct the forces of nature is evidenced in a more ambiguous manner in the following chapter. The psalm-like invocation that frames 42:10-17[35] invites all of creation to break forth in praise of YHWH at the prospect of the "new things" that are repeatedly announced (42:9; 43:19; 48:6). Following a prolonged period of inactivity, where God's face was hidden (42:14), YHWH is about to be stirred into action. But the effect of this dramatic intervention in nature, while reminiscent of the apocalyptic visions of chapter 13, appears to run counter to the creative energies highlighted earlier. Now YHWH's sovereignty over creation is expressed in a program of environmental degradation against Israel's foes (42:13), in which mountains are leveled and rivers exhausted (42:15). Such destructive power asserts the dominion of YHWH over creation and history and preludes YHWH's assertion of power over darkness and the ability to give light to the blind (42:16). Echoing the theme of restoration announced at the outset (40:1), YHWH will lead Israel out of the "furnace of affliction" (48:10) and guide them back from captivity to the land in a festal procession, one in which all creation is summoned to give praise (55:12).

The qualitatively original nature of this song is entirely in keeping with the prospect of the "new things" set out in 43:14-21. In language evoking the Exodus, the prophet seeks to evoke the unity and

---

35. For a similar literary composition extolling YHWH as both king and/or creator, see Isaiah 24:10-12; 44:23; 49:13; and 54:1. See also Psalms 33; 96; 149.

continuity of history in YHWH's purposeful and dynamic will. Rather than a simple expression of the pattern of cyclical repetition which defined much of ancient Near Eastern historical consciousness,[36] what is about to unfold (43:19) is something which is radically new and which will overshadow and surpass the events of old. Thus, while there may well be a correspondence of meaning between the "first" and the "last" things, it is clear that the events associated with the descent into Egypt (52:4) and the eventual creation of a passage through the sea (43:16) are not to be understood as somehow determinative of either God's redemptive powers or Israel's reaction to them. What is presented as new, then, is not confined to an essentially thin interpretation of past events[37] but rather based on a conviction and an awareness of their essential and ever amplifying continuity. For in counseling Israel to "forget the things of old" (43:18) the prophet is advocating not a break with tradition but rather the activation of an appreciation of that tradition's seamless continuity, its dynamism and its vitality. It is the recognition that the creative and redemptive power of YHWH, as the sovereign of history, is characterized by both innovation and renewal, which highlights the character of the "new things." Just as God is truly sovereign, so creation is open-ended and full of potential, a fact testified to on numerous occasions within the work. Incomparable in his commitment to Israel (40:25; 45:5; 46:3-5; 47:8), YHWH's unrivaled work in creation (44:24; 45:12; 48:13; 51:13) is so totalizing as to encompass what are fundamentally opposing phenomena:

> I am YHWH; there is no other,
> who forms light and creates darkness,
> who makes weal and creates woe
> I, YHWH, make all these things. (45:6b-7)

---

36. Rudolf Bultmann, "Ursprung und der Typologie als hermeneutischer Methode," *TLZ* 75 (1950), cols. 206–12. See also Robert K. Gnuse, *Heilsgeschichte as a Model for Biblical Theology: The Debate concerning the Uniqueness and Significance of Israel's Worldview,* College Theological Society (Lanham, MD: University Press of America, 1989).

37. Clifford Geertz, "Thick Description: Towards an Interpretive Theory of Culture," in Clifford Geertz, *The Interpretation of Cultures: Selected Essays* (New York: Basic Books, 1973), 3–33.

Comprising the central verses of what is arguably the most sig-nificant discourse in the entire work,[38] the assertion that YHWH's creative prowess is all-embracing[39] has often been read as either a polemic against proto-Zoroastrianism[40] or a declaration that YHWH is the source of evil.[41] While the first option is unlikely, given the fact that Cyrus is the divinely appointed agent of redemption,[42] the second is simply a mistranslation taken out of context. The second word pair of verse 7 is not good and evil, in a moral sense, but rather weal (*shalom*) and woe (*ra*),[43] which when read in conjunction with the earlier pairing of light and darkness indicate in typical poetic form a concern *not* with the genesis of such pairings but rather with their all-encompassing totality. Do not look for other causes; do not look to other gods, for it is YHWH alone who is "responsible for all these things."

38. Following from the explicit identification of Cyrus as the "anointed of YHWH" (45:1), and sandwiched between the celebration of creation's burgeon-ing influence (45:8), the claim made for YHWH here is among the most com-prehensive in the entire Bible.

39. Though not to be assumed as universally accepted, the claim that YHWH is the source of everything that happens finds echoes in Isaiah 41:23 and Amos 3:6 and 5:18-20.

40. Simon J. Sherwin, "Old Testament Monotheism and Zoroastrian Influ-ence," in Gordon, *The God of Israel*, 113–24.

41. Peter Hayman, "Rabbinic Judaism and the Problem of Evil," *SJT* 29 (1976): 461–76.

42. To this, one should add that there is no evidence that Zoroastrian dual-ism was at this time a recognizable force or that Cyrus himself was a devotee. For an argument to the contrary, see Jason Silverman, *Persia and Apocalyptic: The Transition from Prophecy to Apocalyptic in Second Temple Judaism* (PhD thesis, Trinity College Dublin, 2011).

43. It is certainly true that the Hebrew term רע does carry the primary mean-ing of "evil," as North long ago pointed out; the difficulties created for the modern mind in attributing all events to the agency of God did not arise for the ancients. Although the verse excludes any metaphysical dualism reminiscent of Zoroastrianism, it does embrace both "calamity" and "suffering" as polar opposites to שלום, all of which find their source in God. For a similar under-standing, see Amos 3:6 and Lamentations 3:38; North, *The Second Isaiah*, 151; John Goldingay, *The Message of Isaiah 40–55: A Literary-Theological Commentary* (Edinburgh: T&T Clark, 2005), 268–70.

In eliminating all rival claims, be they those of the Babylonian pantheon or even the potential autonomy of Cyrus himself, the doxological claim of 45:6-7 alerts us to a powerful theme resonating throughout 2 Isaiah: that of *creatio continua*. For while the pairing of both light and darkness within the creative repertoire of YHWH represents a clear allusion to the first act of creation recounted in Genesis 1, the prophet is fundamentally unconcerned with the institution of such primordial phenomena. For 2 Isaiah, creation is not a unique, singular event but rather a dynamic, forceful, and perpetual process.[44] Thus, whereas the creator God of Genesis models the salutary rhythm of work and rest (Gen 2:1-3), the creator of 2 Isaiah grows neither faint nor weary (40:28) but works unceasingly to empower the faint and strengthen the powerless (40:29).[45] This affirmation of the enduring artisan-like qualities of the creator is extended further in 45:18-19 by the assertion that God, the creator of the heavens, did not create the world to be an "empty void." While some read this statement as a veiled polemic against the Priestly account,[46] it is far more likely that the prophet echoes the sentiments of Genesis in proclaiming the destiny of the earth, and Judah in particular, as one of habitation, not desolation.

The assertion that the earth is to be inhabited (45:18), along with the implied invitation to repopulate the abandoned Zion, while bound up with the destiny of Jerusalem under Cyrus,[47] is also

44. This reading of creation in 2 Isaiah as an ongoing activity is given added emphasis by the Hebrew of 45:7 where the verbs ברא (to create) and עשה (to do, to make) are rendered in the active participle form. As Jacob Weingreen notes, "The [active] participle may be regarded as a verbal adjective. . . . Though it expresses the English present tense . . . it indicates a state of continued activity." See Jacob Weingreen, *A Practical Grammar for Classical Hebrew*, 2nd ed. (London: Clarendon, 1959), 66.

45. Michael Fishbane, *Biblical Interpretation in Ancient Israel* (Oxford: Clarendon Press, 1985), 325–26.

46. See, for example, Benjamin D. Sommer, *A Prophet Reads Scripture: Allusion in Isaiah 40–66* (Stanford, CA: Stanford University Press, 1998), 142–43; Moshe Weinfeld, "God the Creator in Genesis 1 and in the Prophecy of Second Isaiah," *Tarbiz* 37 (1967–68): 105–32; 123–24 [Hebrew].

47. Although the expectation that the city destroyed by the Babylonians will be restored under Cyrus is frequently expressed (Isa 45:13; 49:14-21), the

indicative of a profound and intense interest in the regeneration of the earthly sphere of creation. Indeed, one need not look far for numerous references to the rich botanical growth envisioned as either a celebration of the universal sovereignty of YHWH or an accompaniment to the returning exiles.[48] Yet while the prophet's discourse betrays a remarkable familiarity with the botanical diversity of the Syro-Palestinian region,[49] such awareness seems to converge on the image of the Garden of Eden:

> For YHWH will comfort Zion;
> he will comfort all her desolate places,
> making her wilderness like Eden
> her desert like the garden of YHWH. (51:3)

Framed within a series of imperatives which demand of "the righteous" to "listen" (51:1, 4, 7, 21) and to "look" (51:2, 6, 22), chapter 51 calls attention to the blessing of Abraham who, as one man and under the most unlikely circumstances, took possession of the land (51:2). The reason for such a directive is clear: "YHWH will comfort Zion" (51:3). As the defining characteristic of the entire work (cf. 40:1), such *comfort* is again intimately bound up with the anticipated reversal of the pronouncements of the earlier tradition that accented judgment and destruction. In stark contrast to the reduction of Jerusalem to a wilderness and desert (5:17; 6:11; 17:2), under the force of the "new creation" being enacted by YHWH, Jerusalem will blossom like the Garden of Eden and exude the wondrous power of life (51:3). While the repeated announcement of the "new things" (41:20; 45:8; 48:7) recalls earlier events in Israel's history, as Brown has demonstrated, the choice of botanical imagery

---

actual restoration of the temple itself only becomes of concern at a later point as evidenced by Isaiah 63:18 and 64:11.

48. See, for example, Isaiah 41:19; 42:9; 44:14; and 55:13.

49. See Michael Zohary, *Plants of the Bible* (Cambridge, UK: Cambridge University Press, 1983) and Harold M. Moldenke and Alma L. Moldenke, *Plants of the Bible* (London: Routledge, 2002). William P. Brown, *Ethos of the Cosmos: The Genesis of Moral Imagination in the* Bible (Grand Rapids, MI: Eerdmans Publishing Co. 1999), 241–43.

serves to naturalize the miraculous nature of divine activity.[50] The multiple horticultural images, of sprouting (41:19; 44:1-4, 14; 55:10), of the abundance of flora and fauna (41:19), or free-flowing rivers and pools (41:18; 43:20; 44:3; 48:21; 49:10) and of the restorative power of rain itself (45:8; 55:10), indicate not just the divinely or-dained recultivation of the land but a transformation which ulti-mately negates the powers of chaos that threaten any return of the "ransomed" (51:9-11).

In an intensely lyrical conclusion, which communicates unambigu-ously that YHWH's gift of redemption is freely bestowed (55:1),[51] the prophet recalls the programmatic opening statement that Israel's "time of service" is ended (40:2). Israel is called to "go out" (55:12), to commence the new exodus, not in fear and haste, but in comfort, in joy, and in peace. Having submitted to the fact of YHWH's sover-eignty (55:11), having testified to his exposure of the illusory power of empire (40:15), and consequently to his singular status as creator of all (54:5), the final fulfillment of the prophetic message can be envisioned. In a clear allusion to the ancient "curse on the soil" re-counted in Genesis 3:18, all creation gives praise to the new thing being enacted by YHWH.

> For you shall go out in joy,
> and be led back in peace;
> the mountains and the hills before you
> shall burst into song,
> and all the trees of the field shall clap their hands.
> Instead of the thorn shall come up the cypress;
> instead of the brier shall come up the myrtle. (55:12-13)

The thorn and the brier, leitmotifs within the Isaiah tradition for a life diminished by God's judgment (5:6; 7:23-25; 27:4; 32:13),[52] are dismissed and replaced by emblems of growth, of beauty, and of

---

50. Brown, *The Seven Pillars of Creation*, 207.
51. Blenkinsopp has indicated that one may read here a "covert attempt to subvert the standard view of covenant as expressed in classical form in Deuter-onomy" where "God's intervention on behalf of his people is contingent on their moral performance" (Blenkinsopp, *Isaiah 40–55*, 369).
52. Brueggemann, *Isaiah 40–55*, 162.

promise. While one may be tempted to translate the image of ap-
plauding trees (55:12) as a recognition of the triumph of YHWH
over the wanton destruction of empire, it is perhaps more in keeping
with the rhetoric of the work as a whole to view such activity as but
one element in the cosmic, universal dimension of YHWH's "new
thing" (43:19).

5. Interpretive Implications of 2 Isaiah's "Creation" Imagery

The creative word of God emerges as the central theological motif
of 2 Isaiah's promise of salvation and homecoming to the exiled
Judean community.[53] This eschatological message, which holds out
to Israel the promise of a reversal of its current status of political
marginalization and social inferiority, is intimately framed by the
prophet's understanding of one of the foundational events in Israel's
historical understanding, namely, the Exodus. While his is not an
isolated appeal to that tradition,[54] it does provide the vehicle by
which he communicates his conviction that a recognizable and consistent purpose runs through history. This essentially horizontal axis
of historical interpretation,[55] one which juxtaposes the "beginning"
with the "end," is what allows him to present the "new things" not
as some cyclical return to the past, but as the radical consummation
of YHWH's divine plan.

Central to any belief in the purposeful nature of history is the proclamation of YHWH as universal creator. While the sixteen occurrences
of the verb *bara* are some indication of the enthusiasm with which the
prophet articulates this claim,[56] particularly in his attempt to expose
the fallacy of belief in other gods, it is his appeal to creation itself which
anchors his message. Consistently portrayed as the singular accom-

53. Hans Jürgen Hermission, *Studien zur Prophetie und Weisheit* (Tübingen: Mohr Siebeck, 1998), 129–30.
54. See, for example, Hosea 2:14-15; 11:1; Amos 2:9-10; 3:1-2; Micah 6:4; Isaiah 10:24; Jeremiah 2:6-7; 7:22; Ezekiel 20:5-10.
55. Bernhard W. Anderson, "Exodus Typology in Second Isaiah," in *Israel's Prophetic Heritage: Essays in Honor of James Muilenburg*, ed. Bernhard W. Anderson and Walter J. Harrelson (New York: Harper & Brothers, 1962), 177–95.
56. Isaiah 40:26, 28; 41:20; 42:5; 43:1, 7, 15; 45:7 (twice), 8, 12, 18 (twice); 48:7; 54:16 (twice).

plishment of YHWH, creation in 2 Isaiah is, however, no "one-off" achievement. Entirely consistent with his concern to reveal the patterned continuity evident throughout Israel's history, creation is something that transcends the static temporal consciousness behind Genesis. Rather than an event, creation is a *process*, one punctuated by a fundamental sense of novelty that "stretches out" to encompass and define the entire spectrum of space-time. Within this emergent process, *all* dimensions of life, from the celestial bodies to the waters of the earth, from the abundant flora and fauna to the inhabitants of Zion itself (42:5), all share in the faithful, generous, and protective leadership of YHWH; all "delight" (55:2) in the gratuitous abundance which YHWH now offers. This transformation, one entirely contingent on the passion and compassion of YHWH, is what embodies new life for all.

While it is abundantly clear that 2 Isaiah does much more than simply restate the "doctrine of creation" as a means of announcing salvation to the exilic community,[57] it is also clear that this strategic exercise in theological rebranding does not effortlessly lend itself to the requirements of a contemporary environmental agenda. Such a text, which announces the universal validity of God's redemptive capacity in terms of a radical discernment of the potency of past events, is destined to invite conflicting senses of meaning and of importance.[58] Functioning at all times to extol the magnificence of YHWH as cosmic *creator*, the implicit subordination of *creation* to the sovereignty of YHWH and his redemptive activity can, at one end of the spectrum, be read as a warrant for those peculiar brands of pre- and postmillennial pessimism which advocate the abandonment of any concern with an ecological agenda.[59] While such a reading is not an obvious one, the consistent message of 2 Isaiah that creation is

57. See, for example, Robert Murray, *The Cosmic Covenant: Biblical Themes of Justice, Peace and the Integrity of Creation* (London: Sheed & Ward, reprinted 2007).

58. Robert B. Hays, *The Moral Vision of the New Testament* (Edinburgh: T&T Clark, 1997), 1.

59. For a review of the incredibly diverse spectrum of opinion within the American evangelical tradition over environmental issues, see J. Aaron Simmons, "Evangelical Environmentalism: Oxymoron or Opportunity?," *Worldviews: Religions, Culture and Ecology* 13 (2009): 40–71. David K. Larsen, "God's Gardeners: American Protestant Evangelicals Confront Environmentalism, 1967–2000" (PhD diss., University of Chicago, 2001).

under the sole direction of the creator could translate as an invitation to quietism in the face of what is seen as a divinely appointed end and God's plan for a radically new heaven and a new earth. In such a view, environmentalism emerges as nothing other than a mere distraction. Though decidedly less apocalyptic in orientation, such views are nevertheless echoed in James Lovelock's much-celebrated Gaia hypothesis.[60] In a thesis directed squarely at the pretense of contemporary notions of stewardship,[61] Lovelock depicts the earth as a self-regulating system of such complexity as to render any aspirations of human control or management entirely hubristic. Though he himself never claims a full understanding of the intricacies of the system he postulates, the central contention of his project is that any notion of a technological fix to our current predicament is a woefully inadequate, if not dangerously presumptive, exercise in interventionism that runs counter to the unknown aims of a system which has, for millions of years, operated independently of human intercession.[62] It is true that Lovelock is acutely aware of and sympathetic toward the custodial agenda of Christian notions of stewardship; he is, however, equally scathing of the self-appointed physicians who, he claims, know nothing of the patient they seek to restore.

At the opposite end of the interpretive spectrum are those who might read in passages such as Isaiah 45:18-19 a license to continue with humanity's unchecked encroachment upon the natural world. Though clearly lacking the provocative and potentially incendiary vocabulary of Genesis 1:26-28, the express opinion of Isaiah 45:18-19 that the earth is created/re-created for the purposes of habitation can be held out as a warrant for that particular brand of anthropocentrism which White maintains is the very root of our current crisis. For in expanding the realm of human habitation into every conceivable niche of the ecosystem, in developing the industrial

60. James Lovelock, *The Revenge of Gaia: Why the Earth Is Fighting Back—and Why We Can Still Save Humanity* (London: Allen Lane, 2006). See also *The Ages of Gaia: A Biography of Our Living Earth* (Oxford: Oxford University Press, 1998).

61. On the notion of stewardship, see the various contributions in Robert James Berry, ed., *Environmental Stewardship: Critical Perspectives—Past and Present* (London: T&T Clark, 2006).

62. James Lovelock, "The Fallible Concept of Stewardship of the Earth," in Berry, *Environmental Stewardship*, 106–11.

levels of commercial and technological activity required to sustain the modern world, nature emerges as little more than another resource to be exploited in the furtherance of humanity's ambition. Issues of sustainability, of security, and of safety evaporate in the face of short-term financial gain.

Such possibilities by no means exhaust the potential range of interpretations that might draw from 2 Isaiah some form of authorization for an ethical devaluation or neglect of the environment. But the same text holds out equal prospect for a more positive brand of authorization, one which sees within the words of the anonymous prophet a clarion call for accountability and responsibility toward nonhuman creation. Principal among these must be any perspective that seeks to counteract the aggressive commoditization of the environment through the recovery of an affirmative ecological agenda based on the notion of creation as "God's work." While such constructs can be anchored in any number of passages within Isaiah 40–55, which speak of YHWH as originator (40:28), creator (40:26), and architect (54:11-12) of the natural world, *nowhere* does 2 Isaiah specify, either explicitly or implicitly, what pattern our ethical responsibility toward the environment should take. Theocentric language, which seeks to impress upon its audience the greatness of God and to elicit from them praise for God's creative and sustaining activities, is certainly compelling when viewed within the context of the particular cosmological and mythological presuppositions of the sixth century BCE; but when such language is transposed to the ecologically and scientifically aware milieu of the twenty-first century, the notion of "creation's praise," while not an insignificant theological resource, is certainly one in need of some innovative thinking.

In pressing the case for what Horrell has termed an "ecological spirituality,"[63] it is Richard Bauckham who has been to the fore in recent attempts to recover the contemporary significance of the motif of "creation's praise."[64] While he is appreciative of the richly poetic and highly metaphorical language through which the "voice of the

---

63. Horrell, *The Bible and the Environment*, 54.

64. Richard Bauckham, "Joining Creation's Praise of God," *Ecotheology* 7 (2002): 45–59; and *idem, God and the Crisis of Freedom: Biblical and Contemporary Perspectives* (Louisville, KY/London: Westminster John Knox Press, 2002). See

earth" is communicated,[65] particularly in the Psalms, Bauckham's contention that "there is no indication in the Bible . . . that the other creatures need us to voice their praise for them"[66] would appear to be based upon an almost automatic identification of humans as ecologically problematic. Echoing the sentiments of Lovelock, Bauckham's suggestion that "creation worships God just by being itself, as God made it,"[67] inserts into an otherwise sensitive and thought-provoking treatment the rather alarming notion that humans have little, if any, hope of finding solutions to our environmental problems. Though not to be read as endorsing a brand of disengagement from current environmental issues, Bauckham nevertheless forwards a version of *quietism* that runs counter to the very message of our unknown prophet and the entire humanist tradition, which asserts the indissoluble link between humankind and the natural world.[68] Rather than seek to displace humans from the center of the earth's history and in the process accentuate any sense of a culture/nature divide, we must embrace a more sophisticated brand of ecocriticism that demands a multivalent and creative approach to humanity's intimate and encompassing connection with the world.[69] As Pierre Bourdieu has argued, those who have the chance to devote themselves to the study of the world cannot stay neutral or indifferent to those struggles that define its future.[70]

In developing his eschatological vision of a restored and glorified Israel, 2 Isaiah paints a picture of ecological transformation that proceeds in tandem with, rather than in isolation from, human par-

---

also Terence E. Fretheim, "Nature's Praise of God in the Psalms," *Ex Auditu* 3 (1987): 16–30.

65. Norman C. Habel, *The Earth Story in the Psalms and Prophets*, The Earth Bible 4 (Sheffield, UK: Sheffield Academic Press, 2001).

66. Bauckham, *God and the Crisis of Freedom*, 177.

67. Ibid.

68. See Simon Schama, *Landscape and Memory*. See also Mercia Eliade, *The Sacred and the Profane: The Nature of Religion* (New York: Harcourt, Brace & World Inc., 1959), 117–18.

69. Cf. William J. Lines, *A Long Walk in the Australian Bush* (Sydney: University of New South Wales, 1999).

70. Pierre Bourdieu, *Contre-feux 2. Pour un mouvement social européen* (Paris: Raisons d'Agir, 2001), 7.

ticipation. Indeed, in many ways it is a transformation that is entirely dependent on human involvement. Though never advocating an imitation or replication of YHWH's divine vocation,[71] it is clear that the paradigm shift envisioned by 2 Isaiah functions not simply to draw attention to the majesty of the prime mover but to stimulate that conversion of thought and practice which is the necessary precondition for the realization of YHWH's consummative plan (45:22-23). Time and again, the realization of the promised homecoming is presented as contingent upon a return to YHWH and the recognition of his universal sovereignty (40:10-11; 45:22-25; 51:1-8; 55:11). It is only in liberating itself from the distorting and coercive pressures of the geopolitical realm (52:1), and by identifying wholly with the demonstrated authority of YHWH's "arm" in history, that Israel can realize the liberation and comfort announced as the major theme of 2 Isaiah (40:1), a theme which all creation recognizes, celebrates, and shares in. For just as the highest goal of a transformed nature is to glorify God,[72] so too Israel's vocation is to return to and give praise to God (42:12; 55:11). In 2 Isaiah, then, there is no sense of partition or separation between the natural world and human culture but rather a clear and profound sense of indivisibility, one which articulates the intrinsic relationship between the world around us and our perception and appreciation of it as emanating from and glorifying God.

Conclusion

Although clearly devoid of an obvious or explicit ethical imperative directly relevant to our concerns today, there would appear to be, as Horrell suggests, a clear human imperative: to foster the beauty and richness of creation such that the intricate web of life can

71. See, for example, the inauguration speech of President John F. Kennedy on January 20, 1961, where he reminds his audience that for victory against the common enemies of humanity to be realized "God's work must truly be our own." Also see T. S. Putnam, "From That Day Forth," *Vanity Fair* (February 2011): 105.

72. Cf. Dominic Coad, "Creation's Praise of God: A Proposal for a Theology of Non-Human Creation," *Theology* 112 (2009): 181–89.

continue to reflect and to voice the glory of its creator.[73] While un-avoidably implying the dreaded specter of anthropocentricism, it is nevertheless an anthropocentricism that is wholly collaborative as opposed to solitary in its orientation. It presents an image of both human and nonhuman praise as straining forward in an anticipation of that consummation in which the ambiguities of suffering will be eliminated.[74] Isaiah's image of a renewed, rehabilitated, and peace-able nature is one that can function to inspire, to motivate, and to challenge us to overcome the difficulties that confront us. In recog-nizing the essential earth-dependent situation of our existence, it argues for neither disengagement from nor enslavement *of* nature but rather a reorientation of thought and action around a vision that celebrates the goodness and value of all created things as essential for the well-being of the world. In line with Pound's original convic-tion, then, that the function of literature is to refresh and revive the mind of the reader who insists on knowing, 2 Isaiah can be seen to function like that proverbial "ball of light in one's hand,"[75] challeng-ing us to reexamine and to redefine the nature of our relationship with the world in which we live. Not quite the "new religion" envis-aged by White,[76] it is perhaps a means through which we can rethink the value and ultimately the appropriateness of the "old" one.

73. Horrell, *The Bible and the Environment*, 135.
74. Ibid.
75. Pound, *ABC of Reading*, 9.
76. White, "Historical Roots."

Chapter 4

The Liberation of Creation: Romans 8:11-29

Marie Turner

For the ecological reader, Romans 8:11-29 is a remarkable text. It is a text that formulates a theology of creation integrating the Christ-event and the work of the Spirit into a redemptive theology for the whole created world. Nevertheless, a cautionary note is in order because Romans 8:11-29 starts with an ambivalent concept.

1. Flesh and Spirit: Pauline Anthropology

> So then, brothers and sisters, we are debtors, not to the flesh, to live according to the flesh—for if you live according to the flesh, you will die; but if by the Spirit you put to death the deeds of the body, you will live. (Rom 8:12-13)

On first reading, the above text evokes a hierarchical dualism, which apparently denigrates the flesh in opposition to spirit. Such dualistic language is used frequently in the text of Romans 8:3-6, with its series of references to flesh and spirit in oppositional terms. Paul states in 8:6, "To set the mind on the flesh is death, but to set the mind on the Spirit is life and peace." What may be seen as the denigration of the body of flesh, however, needs to be understood in reference to Paul's anthropology.

When Paul speaks of living according to the flesh, he is speaking of human beings living as though independent of God. He is not inferring that the material body is, in itself, somehow evil. Rather, he is reminding his audience that when human beings depend on their own devices without acknowledging their dependence on God, they are courting death, as it were. Luke Timothy Johnson succinctly explains Paul's position, "The problem is not the body, but that attitude of the flesh that lives as though God had no claim on human existence."[1] The language of Paul, therefore, is to be understood not in the framework of hierarchical dualism but in terms of Paul's understanding of redeemed humanity. It is the indwelling of the Spirit that gives life to human beings and makes them "children of God" (Rom 8:6). Paul in fact draws upon the language of "sinful flesh" to articulate his particular approach to the mystery of the incarnation. He says in Romans 8:3-4: "For God has done what the law, weakened by the flesh, could not do: by sending his own Son in the likeness of sinful flesh, and to deal with sin, he condemned sin in the flesh, so that the just requirement of the law might be fulfilled in us, who walk not according to the flesh but according to the Spirit" (8:3-4).

Romans 8:3-4 expresses the Christian claim of the incarnation in terms of Jesus' becoming one with us who are of "sinful flesh." Rather than speaking in oppositional terms, Paul's message is one of unity. The Son partakes of our humanity in the incarnation, in his "becoming sinful flesh." In so doing, he becomes one with the very body of our humanity. Flesh is to be seen, therefore, not as an oppressive burden to be cast off by humankind but as the very means of an existential encounter with the Son.

It is in this flesh that Christ shares in our humanity, subject to all that humanity suffers, excepting sin but including death. As Sandra Schneiders points out in reference to the bread of life discourse in John 6:26-66, in the tradition of Semitic anthropology, "flesh refers not to a part of a dead organism, but to Jesus himself as living mortal. Because he is mortal, Jesus can be killed and therefore become, through his resurrection, the spiritual or living food that gives life

---

1. Luke Timothy Johnson, *Reading Romans: A Literary and Theological Commentary* (New York: The Crossroad Publishing Company, 1997), 123.

to the world."[2] While the Gospel of John, as we have it in its canonical form, is later than Romans, the Semitic background to the Fourth Gospel has been recognized since the publication of the Dead Sea Scrolls. As such, it shares a common cultural understanding with Pauline anthropology. In spite of the fact that when Paul is writing, the resurrection event has already taken place, humanity is still subject to sin and therefore death. This is because Paul conceives of the world as being caught in the eschatological tension between two epochs, that is, the epochs before and after the Christ-event. Until the final fulfillment of God's plan of salvation takes place, the epochs overlap and "sinful flesh" is still a reality and human beings, as all creation, are still subject to death.

2. Paul's Inclusive Soteriology

All Humanity

Throughout the Letter to the Romans, Paul argues for the inclusion of all humanity in the salvific action of God. In Romans 1, Paul makes it clear that God's revelation is available to all humanity, because God can be known through the things of creation. The "universal human being," even without the benefit of God's covenantal revelation, should be able to acknowledge God the Creator from the Creator's work: "Ever since the creation of the world [God's] eternal power and divine nature, invisible though they are, have been understood and seen through the things [God] has made" (1:20). In Romans 4 Paul argues for the inclusion of believers, whether Jew or Gentile, in God's "family." He argues that Abraham was justified by his faith in God because he believed in the promise even before God established the covenant with him. While the inclusion of the Jewish people in the salvific plan of God is clear from the Mosaic covenant, Abraham is the model and precursor for those Gentiles who are outside the covenant people.

All Creation

Thus far, Paul's vision of the all-inclusive nature of salvation concerns human beings. In Romans 8, however, Paul extends his

---

2. Sandra Schneiders, "The Lamb of God and the Forgiveness of Sin(s) in the Fourth Gospel," *CBQ* 73 (2011): 1–29, 25.

vision even to nonhuman creation. This turn of thought is not altogether unexpected when we remember that Paul is deeply rooted in
his Jewish tradition with its many texts lauding God's connection
with God's creative works. The Jewish concept of righteousness is
concerned not so much with "doing the right thing" as with the
relationship which God establishes with the covenanted people of
God and indeed with the whole of creation, since all creation, human
and nonhuman, depends on its relationship with its divine creator.
As Brendan Byrne says:

> In Hebrew biblical thought, the Jewish people thought of
> themselves as bound in relationship to the God who had
> rescued their ancestors from Egypt, cut a covenant with them,
> and forged them as a people. National life and well-being
> depended upon the proper working of this relationship. The
> "righteousness of God" underpinned the fabric of society and,
> indeed, the whole social and cosmic order. God's faithfulness
> could be seen in all aspects of life. The Creator gave growth
> and fertility through the cycle of the seasons. If the rains came
> on time, if the harvest was plentiful, this showed fidelity to
> creation.[3]

3. Romans 8

Romans 8 becomes a paradigmatic New Testament text for an
ecological reading, for here Paul envisages that the redemption won
by Christ incorporates the whole of created existence, human and
nonhuman. Throughout the chapter, trinitarian language emerges.
This is not to say that Paul articulates a full-blown trinitarian theology, but the seeds of the later theology are sown when Paul argues
that into the alienated human situation God (Father) sends the Son
who, by taking on sinful human flesh, "constitutes a new norm and
possibility of life"[4] and in so doing releases the Spirit who becomes
the liberating force of the New Creation: "If the Spirit of him who

3. Brendan Byrne, *Inheriting the Earth: The Pauline Basis of a Spirituality for
Our Time* (Homebush, Australia: St Paul Publications, 1990), 42.
4. Brendan Byrne, *Romans*, Sacra Pagina 6 (Collegeville, MN: Liturgical Press,
1996), 235.

raised Jesus from the dead dwells in you, he who raised Christ from the dead will give life to your mortal bodies also through his Spirit that dwells in you" (Rom 8:11). It is through this Spirit that humanity is liberated from slavery to become children of God and heirs, sharing in the inheritance of Christ, and with him is able to share in his unique address to the Father as "Abba."[5] "For you did not receive a spirit of slavery to fall back into fear, but you have received a spirit of adoption. When we cry, 'Abba! Father!' it is that very Spirit bearing witness with our spirit that we are children of God, and if children, then heirs, heirs of God and joint heirs with Christ—if, in fact, we suffer with him so that we may also be glorified with him" (Rom 8:15-17).

This language of inheritance is especially appropriate, given the Roman addressees of the letter, where themes of adoption as children with rights of inheritance, as opposed to slaves, would resonate with his readers. As Reidar Aasgaard points out, the idea of adoption occurs most frequently in Romans: "In Christ they are no longer in a slavish position under evil powers; rather they have become adult children."[6]

While the language of filiation and inheritance makes sense in connection with humankind, the concept of freedom, introduced in 8:2, is more inclusive: "For the law of the Spirit of life in Christ Jesus has set you free from the law of sin and of death." As the Spirit has freed humanity from sin and death, so also creation is to be freed from futility and decay; thus creation also participates in the redemptive Christ-event.

> I consider that the sufferings of this present time are not worth comparing with the glory about to be revealed to us. For the creation waits with eager longing for the revealing of the children of God; for the creation was subjected [*hupetagē*] to futility [*mataiotēti*], not of its own will but by the will of the one who subjected it, in hope that the creation itself will be set free from its bondage to *decay* and will obtain the freedom of the glory of the children of God. (Rom 8:18-21)

5. "Abba" is the familiar name by which Jewish children addressed their father.

6. Reidar Aasgaard, "Paul as a Child: Children and Childhood in the Letters of the Apostle," *JBL* 126 (2007): 129–59, 138–39.

In these verses, we have one of the clearest statements of the incorporation of nonhuman creation into God's plan in Christ. Before examining these verses in more detail there is an interpretive difficulty that first needs to be explained.

The Agent of Subjection

Because of the lack of clear grammatical pointers in 8:20, it is not clear whether Paul means that it is *God* or *Adam* who has subjected creation to decay. Should the statement be read to mean that God subjected creation to futility with a clear hope that it would be set free from decay through the action of God? Or could it mean that Adam's sin caused death and decay, leaving creation with some vague hope that sin will not have the last word?

Brendan Byrne represents a strand of scholarship that tends toward Adam as the one who is the cause of creation's subjection to futility.[7] Against this view, James Dunn states, "There is now general agreement that 'υπετάγη [*hupetagē*] is a divine passive (subjected by God) with reference particularly to Gen 3:17-18."[8] Other Pauline passages support Dunn's view: "For 'God has put all things in subjection under his feet.' But when it says, 'All things are put in subjection,' it is plain that this does not include the one who put all things in subjection under him. When all things are subjected to him, then the Son himself will also be subjected to the one who put all things in subjection under him, so that God may be all in all" (1 Cor 15:27-28; cf. Phil 3:21; Eph 1:22).

In the Romans text, if Adam is the one who subjected creation to futility, it is difficult to see how he could have subjected it "in hope" (8:20), since Adam himself was already rendered subject to sin and death. It seems preferable therefore, to interpret Paul's words as referring to God as the agent of subjection. When we recognize that God is the one who subjects the earth to futility, our focus alights upon the hope in which creation was subjected; the verse, therefore, has a positive emphasis rather than a negative one.

---

7. Byrne, *Romans*, 260–61. See his detailed discussion of the issues.

8. James D. G. Dunn, *Romans 1–8*, Word Biblical Commentary (Dallas: Word Books, 1988), 470–71.

Subjected in Hope

It is also clear from Paul's extended argument on Abraham in Romans 4 that the hope in which humankind and indeed all creation were subjected is life itself. Earlier in this letter, Abraham is presented as the model of one who was "hoping against hope" (Rom 4:18), and although his childlessness rendered him "as good as dead" (Rom 4:19), he believed "that he would become 'the father of many nations,' according to what was said, 'So numerous shall your descendants be'" (Rom 4:18). The God in whom Abraham trusts is one who has power to bring life from death. Abraham was made the father of many nations by "the God in whom he believed, who gives life to the dead and calls into existence the things that do not exist" (4:17).

Where Abraham's faith brings life, Adam's sin was the cause of death for humankind: "Therefore, just as sin came into the world through one man, and death came through sin, and so death spread to all because all have sinned" (Rom 5:12). Adam's sin also had consequences for creation (cf. Gen 3:17-18), leading to creation's futility (*mataiotēti*; 8:20) and decay (*phthoras*; 8:21). The statement in Romans 8:11-27 reveals the liberating effect the Christ-event has on both humanity, who will be revealed as children of God, and creation that will be liberated from decay.

4. The Old Testament Background

Two Old Testament texts are considered as the background to Paul's thoughts on the connection between sin and death and the converse, eternal life through Christ; these are the book of Wisdom and the book of Genesis, each of which will now be examined.

The Book of Wisdom

One possible influence on Paul's theology of sin, death, and life is the deuterocanonical book the Wisdom of Solomon, where sin and death are explicitly connected. Humanity, according to the sage, is made in the image of God's eternity, but evil people by their words and deeds summoned death ("But the ungodly by their words and deeds summoned death" [Wis 1:16]) and, in association with the devil, allowed death to enter into the world ("For God created us for incorruption [*aphtharsia*] and made us in the image of his own eternity, but through the devil's envy death entered the world, and those who belong to his company experience it" [Wis 2:23-24]).[9]

Although being created for incorruption, humanity has a choice, according to Wisdom; immortality is available only to those who choose the path of righteousness: "giving heed to her laws is assurance of incorruption [*aphtharsias*]" (6:18). This concept of incorruption is expressed again in 8:13 using the word deathlessness/immortality (*athanasian*):[10] "Because of her I shall have immortality."[11] In the Wisdom of Solomon, immortality and image are explicitly attributes of Sophia, who is an icon of God: "For she is a reflection of eternal light, a spotless mirror of the working of God, and an image [*eikōn*] of [God's] goodness" (7:26). The key words of this verse, "image" and "eternity," convey us back to Wisdom 2:22-23, which declares that humanity is made in the image (*eikona*) of God's eternity. "Image" in the Wisdom of Solomon refers to God's wisdom, personified as Sophia, rather than to Adam as in Genesis 1:26-27. Similar language is found in Romans, only now believers are formed in the image/icon of Christ: "For those whom he foreknew he also predestined to be conformed to the image [*eikonos*] of his Son, in

9. The word translated here as incorruption (*aphtharsia*) is from the lemma φθείρω, whose noun form φθορά is used in Romans 8. The verb is quite rare in the LXX, being found only in the deuterocanonical books (4 Macc 9:22; 17:12; Wis 2:23; 6:18, 19), and this verbal link strengthens the likelihood that Paul is drawing upon the theology of the book of Wisdom.

10. Here, the book of Wisdom seems to be drawing on Hellenistic thinking rather than Jewish anthropology. "Epicurean philosophy held that the gods had material existence but lived forever because they were incorruptible. They enjoyed this state of incorruptibility because they were able to feed on ambrosia, the nectar of the gods, which enabled them to overcome the usual forces that dissipate atoms causing material things to decay. So incorruptibility, or immortality, is a divine quality; only God is immortal"; see Mary L. Coloe, " 'The End Is Where We Start From': Afterlife in the Fourth Gospel," in *Lebendige Hoffnung— Ewiger Tod?! Jenseitsvorstellungen Im Hellenismus, Judentum Und Christentum (Living Hope— Eternal Death?! Conceptions of the Afterlife in Hellenism, Judaism and Christianity)*, ed. Manfred Lang and Michael Labhan (Leipzig: Evangelische Verlagsanstalt, 2007), 182.

11. A form of the word deathless/immortal (*athanasia*) is also found in Wisdom 3:4; 4:1; 8:17; 15:3.

order that he might be the firstborn [*prototokon*] within a large family" (8:29).

The Book of Genesis

In presenting his theology of Christ as the "new Adam," Paul looks back to the creation accounts in Genesis. Through Adam, death came into the world, and through Christ, the new Adam, death is conquered: "For if the many died through the one man's trespass, much more surely have the grace of God and the free gift in the grace of the one man, Jesus Christ, abounded for the many" (Rom 5:15).

Francis Landy makes some comments pertinent to our text, dealing as he does with the garden narrative in Genesis in his work on the Song of Songs. In his view, the Genesis text clearly reflects the aftermath of the act of eating from the tree. The curse upon the Earth in Genesis 3:17 is consequential upon an act that was undertaken facilely but will be paid for grievously. Earth becomes the enemy and produces thistles and thorns, a seemingly deliberate act on the part of Earth to make sure that, from now on, the act of eating will be hard toil, and, at the end, all that awaits is a return to that same dust of the Earth. Landy detects an ecological but ironic twist in the return to dust. While death is the only means of escape from toil, the human being finds his/her true being in being "re-integrated with the earth in death."[12] But the irony is that while humanity's true identity is in communion with Earth, at the same time the curse ensures a continued dissociation between Earth and humanity. As Landy says, "Man [*sic*] is taken from the earth and to it he returns; he is the precondition for its fertility and it is cursed for his sake. Death thus restores the original unity of man and the earth, while the curse ensures their continued dissociation."[13] Even the temptation has sinister implications for the fruit of the tree is the product of the earth. This product of the earth leads to disaster and is therefore a means of alienation. In Genesis, eating the produce of the earth is

12. Francis Landy, *Paradoxes of Paradise: Identity and Difference in the Song of Songs* (Sheffield, UK: The Almond Press, 1983), 255. See Landy's chapter, titled "Two Versions of the Paradise Story," which gives a detailed comparison between the Genesis garden narrative and the garden of the Song of Songs.

13. Ibid.

not a gift from God; rather, eating the fruit has meant alienation from both Earth and God.[14]

In Romans, however, Earth is not seen as the cause of alienation among God, humankind, and creation. If we trace Paul's thoughts in the letter concerning the futility into which creation has been subjected, we find from Romans 1 that the human act of idolatry is its primary cause. This futility has been a result of humankind's failure to acknowledge God as creator.

> Ever since the creation of the world his eternal power and divine nature, invisible though they are, have been understood and seen through the things he has made. So they are without excuse; for though they knew God, they did not honor him as God or give thanks to him, but they became futile [*emataiōthēsan*] in their thinking, and their senseless minds were darkened. Claiming to be wise, they became fools; and they exchanged the glory of the immortal God for images resembling a mortal human being or birds or four-footed animals or reptiles. (Rom 1:20-23)

Created things were meant to be a source of revelation, a means of directing humanity to God, but instead of seeing creation as a path *to God*, humankind saw the things of creation *as god*. They became futile (*emataiōthēsan*) in their reasoning, and as a consequence of their rejection of God, God handed up the unrighteous to social disorder (1:24), "because they exchanged the truth about God for a lie and worshiped and served the creature rather than the Creator, who is blessed forever!" (Rom 1:25). The context of the passage is the worship of corruptible/mortal (*phthartou*) images as opposed to the worship of the immortal God. The alienation between God, humanity, and Earth lies in human choices.

5. Creation's Birth Pangs

In Romans 8:22-26, Paul's theology reverses the picture of alienation that Landy so bleakly poses. The series of groanings, which form

---

14. Ibid.

such a striking section of the chapter, represent a reconnection of earth and humankind, reinforced through the prayers and intercession of the spirit. The whole of creation as it groans in travail is connected with humankind and the Spirit through the series of "groanings," thus:

A. [22]We know that the **whole creation has been groaning in labor pains** [*systenazei kai synōdivei*][15] until now; [23]and not only the creation,
B. but **we ourselves**, who have the first fruits of the Spirit, **groan** [*stenazomen*] **inwardly while we wait for adoption, the redemption of our bodies**. [24]For in hope we were saved. Now hope that is seen is not hope. For who hopes for what is seen? [25]But if we hope for what we do not see, we wait for it with patience.
C. [26]Likewise the Spirit helps us in our weakness; for we do not know how to pray as we ought, but **that very Spirit intercedes with** sighs too deep for words [literally, with **unutterable groanings** [*stenagmois*]. (Rom 8:22-26)

The effect of the series of groanings is to bind together creation (v. 22) and humankind (v. 23), with the Spirit as intercessor (v. 26). The groanings become a diminuendo, decreasing in sound until we come to the unutterable groanings of the Spirit.

Several commentators see Genesis 3 as the source of Paul's thought in this section on the travail of creation. As Joseph Fitzmyer points out, Greek philosophers "often compared the vernal rebirth of nature to a woman's travail,"[16] but we should remember the difference between, on the one hand, Greek philosophy which emphasized the dualistic opposition between spirit and matter and the need to liberate spirit from matter and, on the other hand, the Christian approach which wished to liberate matter itself from the bondage

15. According to Newman, *synōdinō* means to "suffer great pain together (as of a woman in childbirth)"; see B. M. Newman Jr., *A Concise Greek-English Dictionary of the New Testament* (Stuttgart, Germany: Deutsche Bibelgesellschaft; United Bible Societies, 1993), 176.

16. Joseph A. Fitzmyer, "The Letter to the Romans," in *The New Jerome Biblical Commentary*, ed. Raymond E. Brown, et al. (London: Geoffrey Chapman, 1990), 854.

into which Adam's sin cast the Earth in common fate with human-kind. Here, the groanings of creation are not a negative concept but the life-giving pains of childbirth, directed toward the coming-to-life of humankind as children of God. Creation is thus depicted as co-creator with God, delivering humankind from death and decay.

Paul knows that death is a reality in the world. For Paul, all have sinned and all fall short of the glory of God. Salvation takes the form of adoption as children of God and the redemption of the body (8:23). The reconciling work of Christ has allowed the righteousness of God to have its liberating, life-giving effect. This life-giving effect is what creation is waiting for: the coming into being of the children of God through adoption.

Johan C. Beker, in a section dealing with Romans 8:17-39 and the "triumph of God," expresses this cosmic theology well. Beker urges Christians to look with the eyes of faith into the created world, a world subject to the bondage of decay. Because of the fall, creation sighs and groans for redemption. In Romans 8:37, "in all these things" (Gk. *en toutois pasin*) refers to the final defeat of the "powers" (8:38). In his apocalyptic reading of Paul, Beker claims, "The God of the End . . . discloses the God of the Beginning." Romans 8:28-30 celebrates God's sovereignty "which is manifest in our predestination to glory through Christ's Resurrection," through Christ as "the first-born" (8:28-30). Beker claims that "Christology here serves theology: it adumbrates God's majestic reign over our world." In this view, suffering is not a tragic flaw "but in some sense serves a purpose in God's triumphal plan."[17] The sufferings of the present will not have the final word, but in the cosmic plan of God, they will be "wiped out" in God's future glory.[18]

6. Romans 8:11-29: An Ethic That Promotes the Flourishing of All Planetary Life

As Paul headed toward Rome, the prospect of death may well have been in his mind. The themes of life, death, and decay, which

17. Johan C. Beker, *Paul the Apostle: The Triumph of God in Life and Thought* (Philadelphia: Fortress Press, 1980), 365.
18. Ibid.

are threaded through the letter to the Romans, indicate that Paul was concerned with the fragility of created existence. In Romans 8:11-29 he constructs a vision of all creation, human and nonhuman, eagerly awaiting the emergence of a champion who would conquer the ultimate enemy, Death. To say that Paul uses the literary vehicles of myth and metaphor to express his theology of the salvation of all things through participation in the death and resurrection of Christ is not to deny its basis in reality. The metaphor works by taking a known referent and comparing it with a deeper mystery, thus signifying the reality that is otherwise beyond expression. In this case, the known referent is the death of the historical man Jesus, while the deeper mystery is the victory over death through the resurrection. Paul begins his letter to the Romans with the statement that Jesus Christ our Lord "was declared to be Son of God with power according to the spirit of holiness by resurrection from the dead" (1:4). With this opening theology, he announces his belief that Christ has conquered Death.

In his self-sacrificial battle through death to resurrection, Jesus has won for all creation forever the hope of life. Paul sets out in Romans to show that salvation is for all. Where the Mosaic Law was the way of identification of all those who belonged to the covenant community, the death and resurrection of Christ opens salvation to all. For the most part, the letter to the Romans argues for the inclusion of Jew and Gentile, and this is the most obvious theme of the letter. But almost hidden away in Romans 8:11-29 is a much wider vision: the inclusion of all creation in the redemptive work of Christ. Mindful of Schneiders' insight that "flesh" in Semitic thought denotes mortality and vulnerability to death, the binding together of humankind and all creation takes on a deeper significance. As mortals created by God, and sharing in the same fate as the rest of creation, we share the same hope of liberation. It is the work of the Spirit, as it groans together with humankind and inanimate creation, to bring this hope of liberation before God. Nonhuman creation groans in its labor pains as it looks toward the glorification of humankind. For humankind's part, to behave in any way that disregards or neglects any part of God's creation would be tantamount to disparaging the all-inclusive nature of Christ's redemptive work.

Chapter 5

Creation in the Gospel of John[1]

Mary L. Coloe

John's gospel resounds with an affirmation of life: "I came that they may have life in its fullness" (10:10).[2] Where the Synoptic Gospels work from a theological framework of sin and atonement, John speaks of life and eternity life.[3] This is an alternative approach to the meaning of Jesus' life, death, and rising that can speak to the heart of human desires today.

The theme of creation is established in the opening words of the gospel with the faith affirmation that all creation had its origins in God, "In the beginning." These words immediately take the reader back to the opening words of the Scriptures and the creation account in Genesis 1. Reading the prologue (John 1:1-18), with an awareness

---

1. This essay began life as a paper given to commemorate the Centenary of the Melbourne College of Divinity in July 2010. That paper was then published as "Theological Reflections on Creation in the Gospel of John," *Pacifica* 24 (2011): 1–12. This current essay is a substantial development of that earlier material.

2. In this chapter, English translations of the New Testament are my own.

3. The phrase *zōēn aiōnion* is usually translated as "eternal life," which can be understood in a temporal sense, as life continuing forever. I prefer to use the expression "eternity life" to emphasize that Jesus offers an entirely different *quality* of life—the life God lives in eternity. This phrase, "eternity life," occurs seventeen times in John, making this a major theme: 3:15, 16, 36; 4:14, 36; 5:24, 39; 6:27, 40, 47, 54, 68; 10:28; 12:25, 50; 17:2, 3.

of Genesis 1, it is possible to see that these eighteen verses are closely modeled on the first chapter of Genesis.[4] The theme of creation returns in the final chapters of John as the author situates the entire passion and resurrection narrative within the iconography of the Garden of Eden found in Genesis 2. The two Genesis creation accounts therefore frame the gospel's narrative and by this structural artistry confirm the gospel's proclamation: "I came that they may have *life* in its fullness" (John 10:10). In commenting on the use of *inclusio* as part of the literary design, Morna Hooker writes, "The correspondence of beginnings and endings is a feature of a great deal of literature, both ancient and modern. . . . Tidy endings often take us back to where we began: a skillful use of what the literary critics call *inclusio* reminds us that it was, after all, the writer's purpose all along to lead us to precisely this point. . . . The end which brings us back to the beginning forms a satisfying conclusion."[5]

This essay will begin by examining the beginning and ending of the Gospel of John to see how these "bookends" situate the theme of creation within the gospel; this will be followed by asking the question, "What are the theological implications of the gospel's narrative structure within our current understanding of an evolving and expanding universe?"

1. The Prologue

The first eighteen verses of John introduce the reader to the major theme and perspective of this gospel. Jesus, the enfleshed Word, has his origins in God (1:1), and, with God, the eternal Word brings forth all creation (1:3). Creation then becomes the dwelling place of the Word (1:14) who enters human history, where some reject him (1:11) but some receive him and through him are drawn into the life of God and become children of God (1:12). This is the basic story line of the following narrative, which begins with the gathering of disciples (1:19-51) and concludes with these disciples, now called

---

4. I first proposed this in an article: Mary L. Coloe, "The Structure of the Johannine Prologue and Genesis 1," *ABR* 45 (1997): 1–11.

5. Morna Hooker, *Endings: Invitations to Discipleship* (Peabody, MA: Hendrickson, 2003), 3–4.

"my brothers and sisters" (20:17), gathered around the risen Jesus (20:24-29), who is still embodied but has passed through death and now transcends the limits of material creation.[6]

The prologue outlines this story line twice, first in reported speech, then at verse 14 the perspective changes and the report becomes a testimony spoken in the first person by those who experience it: "the Word became flesh and dwelt among **us**, and **we** saw his glory" (v. 14); John cried out, "This man was the one of whom **I** said, 'He who comes after **me**, came before **me**, for he was before **me**'" (v. 15); "from his fullness **we** have all received a gift instead of a gift" (v. 16).

Both major parts of the prologue, the report (vv. 3-13) and the first-person testimony (vv. 14-17), can be set out showing how each part follows a similar movement in three stages with parallel themes.

In the first stage, vv. 3-5 speak of life and light shining in the darkness. When story becomes testimony, v. 14 proclaims, "**we saw** his glory." The Word, present as the life force within creation, has become visible; light has brought perception. The second stage moves from seeing to hearing with the witness of John, at first simply told (vv. 6-8), and then John testifies in his own voice (v. 15). The third stage recounts what happened when the Word entered human history. In this stage, we learn of two responses. Some, his own people, did not receive him (v. 11), but some came to believe in his name and these are given power to become children of God (v. 12). When this account becomes first-person testimony we hear of two gifts: the Law given through Moses and a gift called a "true gift" that *we* have received. The parallelism establishes that the "name" referred to in v. 12 is Jesus (v. 17), and the true gift is to become God's children (v. 12). These parallel stages clearly enunciate the pain and conflict of the following narrative. Jesus came to his own people, the children of Israel, who had received the gift of the Law. But in Jesus

6. Along with many Johannine scholars, I consider chapter 21 a later addition to the original narrative that had its ending at 20:21. For a brief discussion on the place of chapter 21, see Francis J. Moloney, *John*, Sacra Pagina 4 (Collegeville, MN: Liturgical Press, 1998), 62–66 and 545–47. Moloney concludes: "There is a crucial element of discontinuity between John 1–20 and John 21 that calls for the former's being regarded as 'the Gospel' and the latter as 'the Epilogue'" (564).

another gift is being offered, "a gift instead of a gift" (v. 16),[7] which some within Israel will accept, but others will choose the Law and not see in Jesus the fulfillment of its promises.

These parallel accounts are introduced by identifying the central "characters" as the Word existing in eternity with God (vv. 1-2).[8] The accounts conclude by identifying the central "characters" again, only now, having told the story of the Word coming into human history, the "characters" are given a human face as the only Son in the heart of the Father.

The structure can be shown schematically as:[9]

Introduction (1-2) *Logos/Theos* in eternity

Part 1 (story told)		Part 2 (testimony)
A (3-5) light	have seen	**A'** (14) glory
B (6-8) John	have heard	**B'** (15) John
C (9-13) 2 responses	have experienced	**C'** (16-17) 2 gifts

Conclusion (18) *Son/Father* in history

7. In ordinary Greek usage, *anti* means "instead of" and *charis* usually means "gift." Therefore, the expression *charin anti charitos* (1:16) should be translated in its Johannine sense as a "gift instead of a gift." Translators frequently impose the Pauline sense of *charis*/grace upon the Johannine text. See the discussion by Ruth Edwards, "'ΧΑΡΙΝ ΑΝΤΙ ΧΑΡΙΤΟΣ' (John 1:16): Grace and the Law in the Johannine Prologue," *JSNT* 32 (1988): 3–6; also Francis J. Moloney, *Belief in the Word: Reading John 1–4* (Minneapolis: Fortress, 1993), 46–47.

8. A very rich study of the "character" of God in the Fourth Gospel is Marianne Meye Thompson, *The God of the Gospel of John* (Grand Rapids, MI: Eerdmans, 2001). On the characterization of the "Father," which subverts the patriarchal understanding of fatherhood, see Dorothy A. Lee, "Beyond Suspicion? The Fatherhood of God in the Fourth Gospel," *Pacifica* 8 (1995): 140–54.

9. For a summary of other ways of structuring the prologue, see Coloe, "The Structure of the Johannine Prologue and Genesis 1," 40-43.

The bipartite structure, shown here, with three sections framed by an introduction and conclusion, is found in the creation account in Genesis 1. In this account, following a brief introduction (Gen 1:1-2), creation happens over seven days. The first three days describe three acts of separation: day 1, light from darkness (vv. 3-5); day 2, waters above from waters below (vv. 6-8); day 3, water from dry land (vv. 9-13). In the following three days, God acts to populate what was created in the first days. On day 4, the darkness is filled with the stars and the moon, while the day is regulated by the sun (vv. 14-19). On day 5, the waters below are filled with living creatures while the firmament above is filled with birds (vv. 20-23). On day 6, land creatures, including humanity, appear on earth (vv. 24-31). These six days bring God's creative activity to an end, "the heavens and earth were finished" (Gen 2:1), and the seventh day is the Sabbath of divine rest. The writer then concludes the account, "These are the generations of the heavens and the earth when they were created" (Gen 2:4a).

The structure can be shown schematically as:[10]

Introduction In the Beginning (1-2)

Separation	Population
A (3-5) light/darkness;	**A'** (14-19) sun, stars
B (6-8) heaven/earth;	**B'** (20-23) birds, fish
C (9-13) land/waters;	**C'** (24-31) animals, humans

Climax: The Sabbath (2:1-3)

Conclusion The generations of heaven and earth (2:4a)

The Johannine prologue thus mirrors the structure of Genesis 1 as the following diagram demonstrates:

---

10. This structure is noted by many scholars; most recently, see Joseph Blenkinsopp, *Creation, Un-creation, Re-creation: A Discursive Commentary on Genesis 1–11* (London: T&T Clark, 2011), 20.

	Genesis			Johannine Prologue	
	Introduction (1-2)			Introduction (1-2)	

Separation	Population		Story Told	Testimony Given
A (3-5) light/ darkness	**A'** (14-19) sun, stars		**A** (3-5) light	**A'** (14) we saw
B (6-8) heaven/ earth	**B'** (20-23) birds, fish		**B** (6-8) John	**B'** (15) I said
C (9-13) land/ waters	**C'** (24-31) animals, humans		**C** (9-13) children of God	**C'** (16-17) we received

Climax: The Sabbath (2:1-3)

Conclusion (2:4a)   **Conclusion** (18)

As the above diagram shows, the parallel structure of the prologue is similar to the structure of Genesis 1, except that the prologue has no seventh day, no Sabbath. According to John's theology, creation was not complete "in the beginning," and we will hear in this gospel that God is still working: "My Father is still working and so am I" (5:17).[11] I will return to this point later.

As well as the structural parallel between Genesis 1:1–2:4a and John 1:1-18, there are other parallels to be noted. Following the brief introductory verses, both passages introduce the theme of light shining in the darkness: "God separated the light from the darkness" (Gen 1:4); "The light shines in the darkness and the darkness has not overcome it" (John 1:5). The opening phrase, "in the beginning," the significance of God's word in both accounts, the initial theme of light, and the structural parallels indicate that the prologue deliberately evokes the first creation account to introduce readers to the gospel narrative.

2. The Hour

The creation theme is particularly significant in the passion/ resurrection narrative.[12] Only in John do we read that Jesus is ar-

---

11. See also "my food is to do the will of the one who sent me and to complete his work" (4:34).

12. In the Fourth Gospel death and resurrection are one event termed the "hour." Death, in Johannine terms, marks an ending for the enfleshed Word,

rested in a garden, "When Jesus had spoken these words, he went forth with his disciples across the Kidron valley, where there was a garden" (John 18:1).[13] Only John narrates that he is buried in a garden, "Now in the place where he was crucified there was a garden, and in the garden a new tomb where no one had ever been laid" (John 19:41). The garden therefore frames the crucifixion and John emphasizes that the cross is in the center, "So they took Jesus . . . to the place called the place of a skull. . . . There they crucified him, and with him two others, one on either side, and Jesus *in the middle*" (19:17-18).[14] The Johannine addition, "in the middle [*meson*]," echoes the phrase in Genesis where God plants "the tree of life *in the middle* of the garden" (Gen 2:9).[15] The evangelist depicts the crucifixion with the iconography of Genesis 2: there is a garden, and in the middle of the garden is the cross, the tree of life, and at the foot of the cross stand a man, the beloved disciple, and a woman, who is never named but called only "woman" (John 2:4; 19:26) and "the mother" (2:1; 19:25), which were names given to the first

---

but this moment is but a transition into glorification. In the words of Karl Rahner, "It is death into resurrection." See Karl Rahner, *Foundations of Christian Faith: An Introduction to the Idea of Christianity*, trans. William V. Dych (New York: Crossroad, 1978), 266. The moment of death is the moment of Jesus' exultation when he passes into the glory he had in God's presence "before the world came to be" (John 17: 5). In what follows, I will use the expression "appearance narratives" to speak of the events recorded in John 20.

13. Mark and Matthew name the place Gethsemane; Luke names it the Mount of Olives.

14. The Synoptic Gospels mention the two criminals crucified with Jesus "one on the right and one on the left" (Mark 15:27; Matt 27:38; Luke 23:33), but only John adds, "and Jesus *in the middle*."

15. LXX: *kai to xulon tēs zōēs en mesōi tōi paradeisōi*. This phrase, "in the middle of the garden," is repeated in Genesis 3:3. Marie-Émile Boismard and Arnaud Lamouille, eds., *L'évangile de Jean*, Synopse des quatre evangiles en français 3 (Paris: Cerf, 1977), 452; Frédéric Manns, *L'Evangile de Jean à la lumière du Judaïsme*, Studium Biblicum Franciscanum Analecta 33 (Jerusalem: Franciscan Printing Press, 1991), 426–27. In Proverbs, the Tree of Life is identified as Divine Wisdom, which is also a striking Christological theme in both the prologue and across the gospel narrative. "She [Wisdom] is a tree of life to those who grasp her" (Prov 3:18). See Ben Witherington III, *John's Wisdom: A Commentary on the Fourth Gospel* (Louisville, KY: Westminster John Knox, 1995).

woman: "She shall be called Woman" (Gen 2:23). "The man called his wife's name Eve, because she was the mother of all the living" (Gen 3:20). These unique features of the Johannine passion, when taken together, suggest a deliberate evocation of the primordial Garden of Eden and a theology of creation.

Following the scene where Jesus alters the relationship between his mother and disciple to one of mother and son, the narrator states that Jesus knew "that all was now finished." Then, after receiving the vinegar, Jesus states, "It is finished [*tetelestai*]" (19:30). The verb *teleō* reiterates God's judgment at the completion of his six days creative work—"thus, the heavens and the earth were finished (*sunetelesthēsan*). . . . And on the seventh day God finished [*sunetelesen*] the work" (Gen 2:1-2).[16] God's work, which was begun in creation, is brought to its completion at the cross as Jesus dies and breathes down the Spirit to the couple standing beneath the cross. In the next verse, we are told that it was the day of preparation before the Passover and the eve of Sabbath, and the narrator notes "that Sabbath was a great Sabbath." In the Hour, Jesus brings the work he was sent to accomplish to its conclusion. Throughout the gospel Jesus had claimed that God was in fact still working (5:17), that the creative work of God had not yet been completed, and that he had been sent to complete (*teleō*) this work (4:34; 5:36; 17:4). In discussing the prologue and its close structural relationship with Genesis 1, I noted that the prologue has no equivalent to the seventh day, the Sabbath, and I made the point that in this gospel God is still working. It is only with the death of Jesus that creation can hear the words "it is finished," and these words usher in the great Sabbath, marking the completion of God's initial creative work that has been in process since the dawn of time "in the beginning" (Gen 1:1).

In the first chapter of Genesis, God's final work on day 6 is the creation of humankind, and this too is Jesus' final act. When he speaks to his mother and the disciple, he changes their relationships. The disciple becomes "son" to the mother of Jesus, and so the disciple is now in a new fraternal relationship with Jesus. The Beloved

16. Martin Hengel, "The Old Testament in the Fourth Gospel," in *The Gospels and the Scriptures of Israel*, JSNTSup 104 (Sheffield, UK: Sheffield Academic, 1994), 393–94.

Disciple is reborn as brother to Jesus and is therefore incorporated into his sonship. Through Jesus' words, the disciple is "born anew" as child of God, as the prologue had promised (John 1:12). The narrator then states that the disciple "took her to his own [*eis ta idia*]" (19:27). This phrase repeats the words of the prologue describing Jesus coming to his own, *eis ta idia* (1:11), and the consequences that some reject him but others receive him and are given "the power to become children of God" (1:12). The phrase "to his own" forms an *inclusio* that looks back to the promise given in the prologue and now marks its fulfillment at the cross. In Genesis 1, God's final act is the creating of humankind in God's own image (Gen 1:26-27); this action leads into God's judgment of creation's completion ushering in the Sabbath (Gen 2:2). From the cross Jesus draws disciples into his own filial relationship with God, creating them anew as sons and daughters of God, and when this has been done, he announces, "It is finished" (John 19: 30), and creation is now ready for its "great [*megalē*] Sabbath" (19:31).

3. The Appearance Narratives

In one sense, the gospel is completed at the cross. The cross is the moment of Jesus' exultation. In death he has been lifted up and glorified. Disciples have now become brothers and sisters of Jesus and children of God, as the risen Jesus confirms when he says to Mary Magdalene, "Go to my *brothers and sisters* and say to them, 'I am ascending to my Father and *your Father*, to my God and your God'" (20:17). This leads to the question about the function of chapter 20 in this gospel. Why is this chapter needed? I will return to this question following the examination of the Johannine account, giving particular attention to some of the details that are not present in the Synoptic accounts.

The First Day

Two time markers are given: the first day of the week (20:1,19) and eight days later (20:26). The first day is the day after the Sabbath, which commemorates the completion of God's creative activity; the first day therefore signifies the start of a new creation. It is appropriate that the narrative begins in darkness (cf. Gen 1:1) when

Mary Magdalene goes to the tomb; as the events unfold, a new day—the first day—dawns. In first-century CE Jewish and Christian writings, the terminology of the "first day" shifted to the "eighth day" to reflect ideas about the eschatological age when God would fulfill all Israel's longings. The "eighth day" terminology is first found in Christian literature in the Epistle of Barnabas (ca. 95–135).

> He further says to them, *Your new moons and Sabbaths I disdain.* Consider what he means: Not the Sabbaths of the present era are acceptable to me, but that which I have appointed to mark the end of the world and to usher in the eighth day, that is, the dawn of another world. This, by the way, is the reason why we joyfully celebrate the eighth day—the same day on which Jesus rose from the dead; after which He manifested himself and went up to heaven. (*Ep. Barn* 15.8–9)[17]

The appearance narrative bears witness to the meaning of the crucifixion for the believers, from John's perspective. In this gospel the focus is more on the impact of the resurrection for the disciples than on its significance for Jesus. The first creation has been brought to its completion in Jesus' death, when he gives birth to a new humanity born of God. The blood and water flowing from the side of the crucified one symbolizes this moment of birth.[18] The birth symbolism was noted by Edwyn Hoskyns in dialogue with a number of ancient commentators. He wrote: "Thus the original believers stand

17. The eschatological "eighth day" also appears in the Jewish apocalyptic source 2 Enoch (first century BCE): "And I appointed the eighth day also, that the eighth day should be the first-created after my work, and that the first seven revolve in the form of the seventh thousand, and that at the beginning of the eighth thousand there should be a time of not-counting, endless, with neither years nor months nor weeks nor days nor hours" (2 Enoch 33.1).

18. On the "birth" symbolism of the blood and water, see Dorothy A. Lee, *Flesh and Glory: Symbolism, Gender and Theology in the Gospel of John* (New York: Crossroad, 2002), 82, 152–59. Ben Witherington writes, "One needs to be aware that in ancient Near Eastern literature the word 'water' can be and is used as a *terminus technicus*, or at least a well-known circumlocution, for matters involving procreation, child-bearing, child-bearing capacity, or the act of giving birth itself." See Ben Witherington III, "The Waters of Birth: John 3.5 and 1 John 5.6-8," *NTS* 35 (1989): 156.

beneath the cross to receive the new birth very literally 'from above' through the Spirit breathed upon them, and through the Water and the Blood poured out upon them. . . . The Water and the Blood [bear witness] to the new birth of the Christians as nothing less than birth from God. The idea of re-creation and new birth therefore underlies St John's account of the death on the cross."[19]

In the resurrected body of Jesus, disciples glimpse the full transcendence of human personhood, now participating fully in the life of God; in *his* resurrection, we glimpse the transcendence that is in process for all creation.

The Garden[20]

The first person to encounter the risen Jesus is Mary Magdalene, and because the tomb is situated in a garden, she thinks the person she sees is the gardener. There is wonderful irony in this appellation, once we realize the overtones of the Genesis garden present in the events of the "hour." Understanding the Johannine evocation of the original garden of Paradise and who the original Gardener was, namely, God who "planted a garden in Eden, in the east" (Gen 2:8), and as a gardener cultivated it (Gen 2:9) and walked in it (3:8),[21]

19. Edwyn C. Hoskyns, "Genesis I–III and St. John's Gospel," *JTS* 21 (1920): 213.

20. In this short essay, there is not the opportunity to give detailed background on the symbolic traditions of the garden. I refer the reader to Manns, *L'Evangile de Jean à la lumière du Judaïsme*, 401–29; Ruben Zimmermann, "Symbolic Communication between John and His Reader: The Garden Symbolism in John 19–20," in *Anatomies of Narrative Criticism: The Past, Present, and Future of the Fourth Gospel as Literature*, ed. Tom Thatcher and Stephen D. Moore, Society of Biblical Literature Resources for Biblical Study 55 (Leiden: Brill, 2008), 221–35. While the gospel uses the term *kēpos*, and not *paradeisos*, which is the term used for the garden in Genesis 2:8, these two words are interchangeable, and the word *kēpos*, to mean the original garden, is found in Ezekiel 36:35 and later Greek translations. On this point, see the arguments of Jeannine K. Brown, "Creation's Renewal in the Gospel of John," *CBQ* 72 (2010): 280; Hoskyns, "Genesis I–III and St John's Gospel," 214; and Manns, *L'Evangile de Jean à la lumière du Judaïsme*, 405–7. Manns also notes a long patristic tradition of associating the garden of Jesus' arrest and burial with the Garden of Eden (402–7).

21. The placing of the Garden of Eden "in the East" also alludes to the rising of the sun, and John notes that Mary Magdalene came to the tomb in the early

Mary's perception that Jesus is the gardener is accurate.[22] The Risen One has passed through death into the glory that was originally his, with God in the beginning. He returns to Mary as the divine Gardener walking in the garden of his creation (John 1:2).[23]

The much-discussed command spoken by Jesus to Mary Magdalene, "Do not touch me" (John 20:17), may also reflect the Genesis motif of Jesus as the "tree of life," discussed above, in reference to the placement of the cross. In Eden, when the woman explains to the serpent God's prohibition about eating from the tree "in the middle of the garden," she adds to God's command the phrase "and you must not *touch* it [LXX: *hapsēsthe*]" (Gen 3:5), where God's original command was simply not to eat of the tree (Gen 2:17). The LXX uses the verb *haptō*, which is the same verb found in John 20:17 (*me mou haptou*). Whereas the first woman's disobedience in touching

---

morning while it was still dark (*prōi skotias*), indicating that she was there as the sun was rising. See Joel F. Drinkard Jr., "East," in *The Anchor Yale Bible Dictionary*, ed. David N. Freedman (New York: Doubleday, 1992), 248. By the first century, the Garden of Eden was located in Jerusalem and identified with the temple as the Book of Jubilees makes explicit: "And he knew that the Garden of Eden is the holy of holies, and the dwelling of the Lord, and Mount Sinai the center of the desert, and Mount Zion—the center of the navel of the earth" (Jub 8:19).

22. "Mary's words are then true, the risen Lord is *ho Kēpouros*, for he is Lord of the Garden, and once more He walks in His garden in the cool of the day, the early morning, xxi, and converses not with the fallen but with the redeemed." See Hoskyns, "Genesis I–III and St John's Gospel," 215.

23. In her fine study of the creation motif in John's gospel, Jeannine Brown also makes the connection between the Garden of Eden and the garden of the resurrection in John 20. She considers that the evangelist is connecting Jesus "to that first gardener, Adam. At this point in the narrative, John implies an Adam Christology." See Brown, "Creation's Renewal," 281. *Contra* Brown, the biblical tradition presents *God* not Adam as the original gardener. It is God who plants the garden (Gen 2:8); in Genesis 13:10 and Isaiah 51:3 there is the phrase YHWH's garden, and in Ezekiel 31:8, "God's garden." As Mariusz Rosik writes, "In the Old Testament, Eden is thought of as a garden in which it is God, himself, who is the gardener." See Mariusz Rosik, "Discovering the Secrets of God's Garden: Resurrection as New Creation (Gen 2:4b–3:24; John 20:1-18)," *Studium Biblicum Franciscanum: Liber Annuus* 58 (2009): 84. Zimmermann ("The Garden Symbolism in John 19–20," 229) also adds that God is explicitly described as a "gardener" (Num 24:6; 4 Macc 1:29).

the tree brought death, Mary Magdalene's obedience brings the Easter proclamation of life as children of God.[24]

Garden and Temple

The primary meaning of God's garden is the dwelling place of God's presence which leads to the association of the Garden of Eden and the temple in much Jewish thought.[25] In Eden, God was present "walking [*hlk:* hitpa''el] in the garden in the cool of the evening" (Gen 3:8). This same verbal form is used to describe God's presence with Israel "walking about in a tent and a tabernacle" (2 Sam 6–7; also Lev 26:12; Deut 23:14).[26] The temple was elaborately decorated with carvings of trees, flowers, and animals to depict the world of nature: cedars, cypress, gourds, olivewood, palm trees, pomegranates, oxen, lions, and a great laver of water. Just as kings in the Ancient East established their palaces surrounded by gardens, so God's temple was to be God's garden.[27]

Adam was placed in the garden to till it and guard it (*abad* and *shamar*); these two terms are usually translated as "serve" and "guard." This same expression is used to describe the ministry of the priests who "serve God in the Temple and guard the Temple from unclean things entering it (Num 3:7-8; 8:25-26; 18:5-6; 1 Chron 23:32; Ezek 44:14)."[28]

---

24. Rosik, "The Secrets of God's Garden," 93.

25. Howard N. Wallace, "Garden of God (Place)," in *The Anchor Yale Bible Dictionary*, ed. David N. Freedman, vol. 2 (New York: Doubleday, 1992), 906. Also, Howard N. Wallace, "Eden, Garden of (Place)," 282.

26. Gregory K. Beale, *The Temple and the Church's Mission: A Biblical Theology of the Dwelling Place of God*, New Studies in Biblical Theology 17 (Downers Grove, IL: InterVarsity Press, 2004), 66.

27. Lawrence Stager describes the lush gardens built by Nebuchadnezzar in Babylon, Queen Hatshepsut's gardens in Egypt, those of the Assyrian king Ashurnasirpal II in Assur, Sargon II and Sennacherib in Nineveh; see Lawrence E. Stager, "Jerusalem as Eden," *Biblical Archaeology Review* 26, no. 3 (2000): 36–47. Rosik ("The Secrets of God's Garden," 82–83) also describes the significance of the garden for burial sites for kings in the Ancient Middle East.

28. Beale, *The Temple and the Church's Mission*, 66–67. Beale (66–80) suggests eight other points of correspondence between the Garden of Eden and temple based on linguistic and conceptual parallels.

In the Gospel of John, one of the primary Christological symbols of Jesus' identity and mission is that of the temple. In chapter 2 Jesus identifies himself as the temple when he states, "Destroy this temple, and in three days I will raise it up" (2:19), and then the narrator explains, "He spoke of the temple of his body" (2:21). This temple symbolism then continues across the gospel narrative, particularly within the great temple festivals of Tabernacles (John 7, 8, 9) and Dedication (10:22-42).[29] Within the gospel narrative, the evangelist frequently juxtaposes Jesus and the temple; such juxtaposition is not simply providing a location for Jesus' words and actions but must be seen as part of the Johannine theological strategy, presenting with artistic irony that Jesus is the new temple.[30] The situating of the first appearances of the risen Jesus within a garden continues this narrative strategy, only now the temple is depicted in terms of the garden of Paradise.

Eschatological Gifts: Peace and the Spirit

When Jesus comes to the disciples, his first words are "Peace." The Hebrew word *Shalom* means far more than what is conveyed by its English translation, "peace." *Shalom* in the Old Testament carries the sense of wholeness, or completion,[31] and is derived from the

29. I have argued elsewhere on the significance of the temple in the Fourth Gospel and shown how one temple is destroyed in the passion narrative and, at the same time, a new temple is raised. See Mary L. Coloe, *God Dwells with Us: Temple Symbolism in the Fourth Gospel* (Collegeville, MN: Liturgical Press, 2001); "Raising the Johannine Temple (John 19:19-37)," *ABR* 48 (2000): 47–58; "The Nazarene King: Pilate's Title as the Key to John's Crucifixion," in *The Death of Jesus in the Fourth Gospel*, ed. Gilbert Van Belle (Louvain: KUL Press, 2007), 839–48.

30. Manns comments: "The importance of the symbolism of the times and places in the Fourth Gospel has been noted many times. John's details are never supplied gratuitously. They are inserted into a network of meanings that the exegete must evaluate if he wants to educe the theological scope of a scene." See Manns, *L'Evangile de Jean à la lumière du Judaïsme*, 401.

31. "In one form or another, the notions of wholeness, health, and completeness inform all the variants of the word." See Joseph P. Healey, "Peace," in *The Anchor Bible Dictionary*, ed. David Noel Freedman, vol. 5 (New York: Doubleday, 1996), 206; also Gerhard von Rad, "שָׁלוֹם in the O.T.," in *Theological Dictionary of*

word *shalem*, to be completed.[32] Thus, there is continuity between the final words of Jesus on the cross, "*tetelestai*, it is finished," and the first word of the risen Jesus, "Peace." In the Hebrew and Greek Old Testament, the term also has a sense of God's final eschatological salvation.[33] The word looks not only back to what has been brought to completion but also ahead to a future fulfillment. From his study of the use of the term "peace" in the Old Testament and rabbinic usage, Werner Foerster concludes: "εἰρήνη thus acquires a most profound and comprehensive significance. It indicates the eschatological salvation of the whole man [*sic*] which is already present as the power of God. It denotes the state of the καινὴ κτίσις [new creation] as the state of definitive fulfillment. In this sense salvation has been revealed in the resurrection of Jesus."[34]

When Jesus repeats his greeting, "peace," he breathes on the disciples and says, "Receive the Holy Spirit" (20:22). The word translated "breathed" (*enephusēsen*) recalls God's action in the garden of Genesis when God formed an earth creature from the dust and then "breathed [*enephusēsen*] into his face" the breath of life, and the earth creature became a living being.[35] When Jesus comes to his disciples and greets them the first time with, "Peace," this could be understood as saying: God's first creation has been brought to completion. When he says to them again, "Peace," and breathes on them the Holy Spirit, this is an act of new creation, reaffirming Jesus' words and actions at the cross. The words of Jesus and the gift of the Spirit on Golgotha constituted the disciple as a child of God, drawing the disciple into Jesus' sonship. In the appearance narratives, the "hour" of Jesus continues, and when the group of disciples are gathered, the Spirit is breathed and the disciples are sent into the world, "As

the New Testament, ed. Gerhard Kittel, Geoffrey William Bromiley, and Gerhard Friedrich (Grand Rapids, MI: Eerdmans, 1964–76), 2:402–6.

32. Robert L. Thomas, "שָׁלֵם, Shalem," in *New American Standard Hebrew-Aramaic and Greek Dictionaries: Updated Edition* (Anaheim, CA: Foundation Publications, 1998), H7999.

33. Werner Foerster, "Εἰρήνη," in *Theological Dictionary of the New Testament*, ed. Gerhard Kittel, Geoffrey William Bromiley, and Gerhard Friedrich (Grand Rapids, MI: Eerdmans, 1964–76), 2:412.

34. Foerster, "Εἰρήνη," 414.

35. Zimmermann, "The Garden Symbolism in John 19–20," 233–34.

the Father sent me, even so I send you" (20:22). There are not two bestowals of the Spirit. I would rather speak of two moments within the *one* Hour,[36] one moment where the focus is on the believer's relationship to Jesus, and a second moment where the focus is on the believer's relationship to the world, as the agent of Jesus in the world.[37] For this reason the narrative describes two moments in the giving of the Spirit to the believers, a moment of birth at the cross (19:30) and a moment of mission (20:21-23).

4. Creation and Re-Creation: Theological Implications

Recognizing the significance of beginnings and endings, Morna Hooker notes, "Beginnings and ends not only belong together but also point forward and backward to the significance of the story that lies in-between."[38] In immersing the story of Jesus within the themes of original creation and eschatological re-creation, this gospel proposes a soteriological perspective that focuses on life and its fullness. This is made explicit in the words of the Johannine Jesus, "I came that they *may have life* in its fullness" (John 10:10); also in the concluding words of the evangelist, "These things are written that you may believe that Jesus is the Christ, the Son of God, and that believing you *may have life* in his name" (John 20:31). Other New Testament writings provide a range of different images in an attempt to answer the question, "What was God doing in the Jesus event?" Paul makes use of first-century Jewish and Hellenistic images to speak of justification, redemption, expiation, reconciliation,

---

36. The unity in the hour of the crucifixion (chaps. 18–19) and the resurrection (chap. 20) is evident in the Johannine insistence that the day of death is a day of "Preparation." Death is not the end but is the essential preparatory stage leading to the dawn of the eschatological "eighth day."

37. For a very clear discussion on the use of *apostellein* and *pempein* as they apply to Jesus and the disciples, see Garry H. Burge, *The Anointed Community: The Holy Spirit in the Johannine Community* (Grand Rapids, MI: Eerdmans, 1987), 200–204. Even in this missioning moment, the creation theme is still present in the New Testament, *hapax legomenon, enephusēsen*, referring to Genesis 2:7 as discussed above. On this, see also Hengel, "Old Testament," 391.

38. Morna Hooker, *Endings: Invitations to Discipleship* (Peabody, MA: Hendrickson, 2003), 267.

salvation;[39] in the rending of the temple veil Mark suggests a theology of atonement (15:38), and this imagery is repeated in Matthew (26:51) and Luke (23:45). Joseph Blenkinsopp considers that "it is no exaggeration to say that the contest between Jesus and Satan is the leading theme in the Synoptic Gospels."[40] The Pauline and Synoptic imagery have dominated Western theology leading to a very narrow focus on the human person and sin, while Anselm's theory of satisfaction has given rise to horrific images of a vengeful God. A study of Johannine soteriology may provide a much-needed alternative that is more attentive to the cosmological significance of the Christ-event and thus more coherent for the twenty-first-century person. Johannine soteriology will focus on re-creation as the "primary explanation of Christian experience."[41]

A Johannine soteriology will necessarily understand the presence of the Word within creation from its beginning (John 1:1-3). From this it follows that the incarnation of the Word is an irruption and manifestation of the divine presence already at work within the whole of creation and human history.[42] In announcing that the Word became flesh (*sarx*), the divine action is not narrowed to humanity but is extended to include the entire created reality. Here it is important to note that "flesh," in the biblical usage, is not simply what today we name in biological terms as a substance common to animal life and therefore excluding inanimate creation; flesh, as understood within the Old Testament, is that aspect of creation that denotes finitude in contrast to God's eternity. "As creature of God he [the human person] is flesh, always exposed to death. . . . Man is

---

39. Joseph Fitzmyer identifies ten different Pauline images used to speak about the "effects of the Christ-Event"; see Joseph Fitzmyer, "Pauline Theology," in *The New Jerome Biblical Commentary*, ed. Raymond E. Brown, Joseph A. Fitzmyer, and Roland E. Murphy (London: Chapman, 1990), 1397–1402.

40. Blenkinsopp, *Creation, Un-creation, Re-creation*, 187.

41. Hoskyns, "Genesis I–III and St John's Gospel," 216, also 218.

42. A recent book by Denis Edwards points out that the link between creation and incarnation was central to the theology of Athanasius. Denis Edwards, *How God Acts: Creation, Redemption and Special Divine Action* (Hindmarsh, S.A.: Australian Theological Forum, 2010), 109–13. Edwards's work has been particularly helpful in my articulating a small part of the theological ramifications of John's creation/re-creation theme.

understood in terms of his relationship, not his nature. He is what he is in relation. Thus flesh is his situation before God."[43] Flesh is that which is bound by time and destined to end, in contrast with the eternal being of God. "All flesh is grass and all the glory of humanity as the flower of grass. The grass withers and the flower fades but the Word of our God abides forever" (Isa 40:7-8). Rudolf Schnackenburg explains the term flesh (*sarx*) thus: "It expresses that which is earth-bound (3:6), transient, and perishable (6:63) . . . in contrast to all that is divine and spiritual."[44] While it is true that the biblical authors were not thinking in terms of modern cosmology or modern biology, it is not inappropriate to extend the meaning of "flesh" to include all that is perishable, that is, all the cosmos governed by the natural laws of decay, entropy, and death; "flesh," and therefore the consequences of the incarnation of the Logos, needs to include all created reality—*ta panta* (see John 1:3; 3:35; 13:3; 16:15; 17:2; 17:10; 19:28).

A Johannine soteriology will therefore necessarily consider the meaning of the incarnation for all creation and not restrict its meaning to dealing with human life. Here, we could learn much from some of the earliest commentators such as Origen, who, in his commentary on John 1:4, wrote: " 'That which has come into being in him,' that is the Logos, 'was life,' in order that just as God brought the universe [*ta panta*] into being, so also what has been created to live might be given life by sharing in him [the Logos]" (*Comm Joh* Catena frag 2).[45]

43. Eduard Schweizer, "Σάρξ," in *Theological Dictionary of the New Testament*, ed. G. Kittel, G. W. Bromiley, and G. Friedrich (Grand Rapids, MI: Eerdmans, 1964), 7:123.

44. Rudolf Schnackenburg, *The Gospel according to St. John*, trans. K. Smyth, et al., 3 vols., Herder's Theological Commentary on the New Testament (London: Burns & Oates, 1968–82), 1:267. For a brief summary of various aspects of Johannine anthropology, see Sandra M. Schneiders, "The Resurrection (of the Body) in the Fourth Gospel," in *Life in Abundance: Studies of John's Gospel in Tribute to Raymond E. Brown*, ed. John R. Donahue (Collegeville, MN: Liturgical Press, 2005), 170–73.

45. As cited in John N. Suggit, "Jesus the Gardener: The Atonement in the Fourth Gospel as Re-creation," *Neotestamentica* 33 (1999).

Johannine soteriology will also need to describe the effect of the Christ-event on human creation not solely in terms of sin but in terms of "re-creation," as suggested by the garden iconography of Genesis 2, or "re-birth" (John 3:5), as indicated by the transformation of the Beloved Disciple to brother of Jesus and child of God, and signified by the flow of blood and water. The disciple, reborn as a child of God, is now gifted with a new quality of life as lived by God in eternity, what this gospel terms "eternal life." Within Eastern Christianity, humanity's participation in the life of God is spoken of as *theosis*, or deification.[46] For Athanasius, incarnation was the means of bringing about the transformation of humanity into the divine image, as John Suggit notes, "the essential fact for him was that the Logos 'became a human being in order that we may be made divine' " (*De Incarnation* 54:3).[47] A return to the Johannine gospel and other ancient writings (*ressourcement*) may provide a new and better language to speak of the Christ-event within an evolutionary and cosmic consciousness. Among Catholic theologians, the work of Denis Edwards draws upon the work of the early patristic writers as well as the more recent work of Teilhard de Chardin and Karl Rahner. While these modern theologians draw upon methodologies proper to their discipline, their conclusions resonate with my biblical exegetical study of the Fourth Gospel. Edwards writes:

46. Irenaeus is thought to be the clearest exponent of this thinking: "The Word of God, our Lord Jesus Christ, who did, through His transcendent love, become what we are, that He might bring us to be even what He is Himself" (*Adversus Haeresis* 5. pref.). Western Theologians are now giving more attention to this ancient Eastern terminology. Denis Edwards writes on redemption as "Deifying Transformation"; see Edwards, *How God Acts*, chapters 7 and 9; also Michael J. Christensen and Jeffery A. Wittung, eds., *Partakers of the Divine Nature: The History and Development of Deification in the Christian Tradition* (Grand Rapids, MI: Baker Academic, 2007); and Stephen Finlan and Vladimir Kharlamov, eds., *Theōsis: Deification in Christian Theology* (Cambridge, UK: James Clarke & Co, 2006).

47. Suggit, "Jesus the Gardener," 165. In his controversy with the Arians, Athanasius states, "For he took to himself a created human body, in order that as a craftsman he might renew it and make it divine in himself. . . . In that flesh he has become for us the beginning of a new creation" (*Arian.* 2.70).

Along with this Eastern theology, Rahner sees salvation as ontological rather than juridical, understands salvation as deification that involves human beings and with them the whole creation, and sees the resurrection of Christ as the beginning of this divinizing transformation. He thus locates a basis for something like the Teilhardian vision in the theology of great Eastern thinkers like Irenaeus and Athanasius.[48]

5. Conclusion

The theme of creation and new creation frame the narrative of the Fourth Gospel. Jesus is announced as the *logos*, present with God "in the beginning," and the "hour" brings God's first creation to its conclusion and ushers in the birth of a new creation. The appearance narratives witness to the beginning of this new creation when materiality is glorified in the risen body of Jesus, promising that what has begun in Jesus is already in process (1) for disciples who have been divinized in becoming children of God, and (2) for all creation that had its origins in the Word and now, through the eternally embodied Word, looks to its final transformation in God.[49]

48. Denis Edwards, "Teilhard's Vision as Agenda for Rahner's Christology," *Pacifica* 23 (2010): 244.

49. For a recent approach to the meaning of the resurrection for all matter, see Edwards, *How God Acts*, esp. chap. 9.

Chapter 6

Christ and Creation: Logos and Cosmos[1]

Anthony J. Kelly

This chapter treats of distinctive Christian and theological elements in the experience and understanding of creation. John's classic statement on the incarnation is central to our exploration: "the Word became flesh and lived among us" (John 1:14). The Word, the *Logos*, is related to the cosmos of our experience as the luminous field in which everything comes into being, so as to participate in the one cosmic order of divine creation.

1. The Logos and the Cosmos: Theological Basis

The Christian perspective on creation can be suggested by referring to some key passages from the prologue of John's gospel:[2]

---

1. This chapter is a much revised and expanded form of a section of my book, *An Expanding Theology: Faith in a World of Connections* (Sydney: E. J. Dwyer, 1993); now out of print.

2. For a fuller theological consideration of the prologue, see John Macquarrie, *Jesus Christ in Modern Thought* (London: SCM Press, 1990), 105–22. Macquarrie's own translation of this passage, especially his use of "meaning" for *Logos* is particularly imaginative. For further discussion, see Anthony J. Kelly and Francis J. Moloney, *Experiencing God in the Gospel of John* (Mahwah, NJ: Paulist, 2003), 29–60.

> In the beginning was the Word [*Logos*], and the Word was
> turned toward God, and what God was the Word also was.
> He was in the beginning with God. All things [*panta*] were
> made through him, and without him nothing was made. (John
> 1:1-3)[3]

Such a passage brims with promise as we read it in the present
context of the twenty-first century. How might this *Logos* embrace in
its meaning all the other *logoi* (meanings) of our human explora-
tions—eco*logy*, cosmo*logy*, and all the *dia-logues* that result? For John,
it seems clear enough that the Word possesses an inexhaustible and
universal originality. As the divine self-utterance, the Word, through
whom "all things" came into existence, is all-creative and all-inclusive,
and "all things" depend on the Word's agency for their intelligibility
and existence.

Though there is a rich historical and philosophical context of association informing the meaning of the *Logos* in John's gospel, the
dominant influence on John's theology of the Word is Jewish theology.
Within that religious frame of reference, the divine Word was understood in active, concrete terms and intimately connected to the Spirit
or Breath of God, as God acted in history. For example, like the divine
utterance of Genesis, John's Word is "in the beginning" (John 1:1;
Gen 1:1); it is all-creative; it overcomes the darkness of chaos and
gives life. It is also linked to the personified, all-pervasive, and governing "wisdom" of the Sapiential literature (Prov 8:22-31; Sir 24).
This concrete, historical emphasis culminates in the prologue itself
as the Word becomes flesh and "dwells among us" (John 1:14). The
following verses suggest the full scope of the Word in relation to
creation as a whole: "All things were made through him, and without
him nothing was made. What took place in him was life, and the life
was the light of humankind. The light shines in darkness, and the
darkness has not overcome it" (John 1:3-5).

As the prologue now unfolds into the sphere of creation, the
primordial Word is of focal significance. God is presented immedi-

3. This translation of the Johannine prologue (1:1-18) follows Francis J. Moloney, *The Gospel of John*, ed. Daniel J. Harrington, Sacra Pagina 4 (Collegeville,
MN: Liturgical Press, 1998), 33. Hereinafter, I use the Moloney translation.

ately not as creator but as *God-in-communion* with the Word, communicating on the uncreated level of divine life and being. For the Word "was in the beginning with God" (John 1:2). Out of this communion and communication, there results the existence of the universe: "all things were made through him, and without him nothing was made" (John 1:3).

Since "the Word was turned toward God" (John 1:1b), the original communication and self-utterance that the Word is transcends all modes of human conversation. In the vocabulary of faith, the *meaning* of "God" begins from and returns to this Word, who is "with God" in the beginning. Nonetheless, the Word is not an abstract principle but "he," *this one* (1: 3-4, 10-11). An actual, addressable subject is implied: one whose original identity will unfold only in the conversational world of human subjects. The people he meets, confronts, and calls will know him as "you," and through all the ages of history refer to him as "he," Jesus of Nazareth. Here too later theology and doctrinal definitions will turn to the question of how there can be one subject belonging both to the divine realm of being and to the realm of finitude and humanity. Previous notions structured on a great dividing line between God and creation will be relocated in a new horizon opening around "one and the same Our Lord Jesus Christ" who is "one in being with the Father as to the divinity and one in being with us as to the humanity."[4] Thus, the falsely limiting options of Docetism, Arianism, Nestorianism, and Monophysitism are transcended. When *this one* who is the Word acts, speaks, prays, and suffers in the person of Jesus, "what God was" (1:1c) from the beginning is invoked, engaged, and revealed.

"All things were made through him" (1:3a): despite the differences existing among all created things, and despite their difference, even alienation, from God, the *Logos* is the genetic and unifying principle of the universe. The diversity of creation is a "uni-verse"

4. Josef Neuner and Jacques Dupuis, eds., "The Symbol of Chalcedon," in *The Christian Faith in the Doctrinal Documents of the Catholic Church* (London: Collins Liturgical, 1982), #614, p. 154. As the fathers of Chalcedon expressed it, "He is one and the same only-begotten, God the Word, the Lord Jesus Christ, as formerly the prophets and later Jesus Christ have taught us about him and has been handed down to us by the Symbol of the Fathers" (ibid. #611, p. 153).

because of its origin and coherence in the Word. *All* creation is a field of divine communication, being "Word-ed" into being. This is the fundamental "logic" of the gospel: nothing has meaning outside the divine *Logos*. Nothing and no one stands in its own right outside the primordial Word.[5]

The *Logos*, by reasons of his origin, incarnation, and mission, creates a *dia-logical* space in which Jesus will enter into conversation with all the range of *dramatis personae* who will populate the dramatic unfolding of the gospel narrative. Addressed by this Word, they will evince either acceptance, incomprehension, hesitation, doubt, questioning, rejection, or any combination of such attitudes. The Word, dwelling among us (John 1:14b), thus opens a unique field of communication. The "God-ward" (*pros ton theon*) status of the Word in the first verse of the prologue presumes a certain dialogical dimension within the divine mystery itself. Coming out of this original communion, the Word enters creation to make it an expanding field of dialogue and communication with others.[6] Into such a conversation, the Word is uttered, and the various actors of the gospel drama are drawn into a dialogue originally existing between the Word and God. As this process reaches out to include believers of every age, God's unrestricted love for the world (John 3:16) provokes the full play of human conversation as it turns on the meaning of life, of God, of creation, of human identity, and on the destiny of the world itself.[7]

In traditional philosophical thinking, the human mind, through its immersion in creation, moves from what it can immediately experience and express to a clouded knowledge of the creative mystery from which all things have come. In the prologue of the gospel, such a pattern is reversed. The Word is presented as the first in meaning

5. Thomas Aquinas, *Summa Theol.*, I, q. 34, a. 3: "Because God understands both himself and all things in one act, the single divine Word is expressive, not only of the Father, but also of all creatures."

6. In reference to an influential Jewish philosophy of dialogue, see L. Augustine Brady, "Martin Buber and the Gospel of John," *Thought* 201 (1978): 283–92.

7. For the hermeneutical (and human) importance of the play of conversation, see David Tracy, *The Analogical Imagination: Christian Theology and the Culture of Pluralism* (London: SCM, 1981), 101, 446–55; *Pluralism and Ambiguity. Hermeneutics, Religion, Hope* (San Francisco: Harper and Row, 1987), 16–27.

from which all subsequent meanings derive. All other *logoi*—words, sciences, philosophies, and theologies—are radically referred to this *Logos*.[8] And yet we are confronted with a paradox at this point. How is the Word to be known, since he is turned to God in the beginning and we human beings are not? The answer must wait on what theology refers to as to the incarnation of the Word (1:14). In this case, of divine communication, the Word is at once like and unlike what falls within the range of our experience. While human and religious preconceptions will be repeatedly challenged in the light of a new realm of experience, there remains a likeness through which the Word becomes accessible to the consciousness of faith. For the Word becomes flesh (John 1:14); the Word enters the world of words and deeds which make up the flesh of our existence. The Word becomes flesh, and the flesh becomes a story. As the gospel will show, that story is made up of the conversations of Jesus with all the variety of those who receive or reject him. Consequently, all the human conversations about who God is and what God wills are set in the context of the Word spoken and speaking "among us" (1:14). The extremes of enclosing God and creation within the sameness of human experience, on the one hand, and the sense of an unbridgeable gulf permitting no communication between God and the world, on the other, are met with the Johannine alternative. The ultimate meaning of God and the radical meaning of the universe are intelligible only in reference to the incarnate *Logos*. The knowledge of faith is, therefore, in the deepest sense, "ana-*logical*."

This does not mean that creation is downplayed when its meaning and existence are centered in the divine Word. What it does mean, however, is that the true character of creation can be known only in reference to the Word in whom the universe came to be. It is brought to fulfillment only when that Word is fully incarnated in the flesh of creation, when Jesus cries out on the cross, "It is finished"

---

8. The relationship of the *Logos* to the *logoi* of creation is one aspect of the great cosmic vision of Maximus Confessor. See Lars Thunberg, *Man and the Cosmos: The Vision of Maximus the Confessor* (Crestwood, NY: St Vladimir's Seminary Press, 1985); for texts and critical comment, see Andrew Louth, *Maximus the Confessor* (London: Routledge, 1996).

(John 19:30a).[9] Furthermore, the Word, as the light of all (John 1:4, 9), constitutes human identity in a holistic relationship both to *God* from whom he comes and to the *"all things"* he creates and illumines. Since the Word is turned toward God, all that has been worded into being and life and light in him are drawn into his God-ward "turning." The Word is inscribed into the existence of all that is, just as all creation communicates in him, in whom it originates, coheres, and converses: "He is the image of the invisible God, the firstborn of all creation; for in him all things in heaven and on earth were created, things visible and invisible, whether thrones or dominions or rulers or powers—all things have been created through him and for him. He himself is before all things, and in him all things hold together" (Col 1:15-17; NRSV).

This experience will lead to a vision of heaven made open, and "the angels of God ascending and descending upon the Son of Man" (John 1:51). Once the Word has become flesh, the horizons of past history are reoriented in the light of this unique event of God's self-revelation. There is nothing on the outside of this event. Everything and everyone is enfolded in the creative Word. There is no originally exterior darkness, no zone of existence outside the domain of the Word. It will appear also, because of "the life that took place in him" (John 1:3-4), that there is even no clear disjunction between life and death (cf. John 6:47, 50, 54, 57-58; 11:26). Even the ostensibly clear metaphors of "up" and "down," "from above" and "from below," must now be refocused in the event of the Word become flesh, dwelling "among us" (John 1:14). The primeval struggle between darkness and light is given a new sense through the primordial light already in the world (John 1:5). Most important, there is no separation between what God is and what the Word has revealed, for that too has been transcended in the statement, "and what God was the Word also was" (John 1:1c).

Likewise, any traditional distinction of flesh from spirit is called into question. The flesh is already included in the genetic totality of

---

9. James Alison and Gil Bailie both make telling points regarding the Johannine sense of creation. See James Alison, *Raising Abel: The Recovery of Eschatological Imagination* (New York: Crossroad, 1996), 72–74, and Gil Bailie, *Violence Unveiled: Humanity at the Crossroads* (New York: Crossroad, 1997), 219–28.

"all things" coming to be in the Word. For flesh is what that same Word has become. Likewise, "faith and reason" are no longer mutually exclusive. Through the Word and its light, such a dichotomy yields to another economy of knowing: "The true light that enlightens everyone was coming into the world" (John 1:9), to be "the fullness of a gift that is truth" (John 1:14a). Furthermore, the conflict of divine and human freedoms, no matter how dramatic and seemingly terminal that conflict appears as the gospel unfolds, occurs in the spaciousness of a universe cohering in the Word who is the light and life of all. The creative Word enters into a world of created freedoms (1:11-13), as addressed to freedom and for the sake of freedom. The disciples of Jesus will not only "know the truth" (John 8:32a), but "the truth will make you free" (John 8:32b). In the "Word-ed" universe, freedom is a reality that will come to its own fulfillment: to those who believe in him, he gives "the power to become children of God" (John 1:12).

Genesis recounts how human beings had, in their pride, once aimed "to build ourselves a city and a tower with its top in the heavens; otherwise we shall be scattered abroad upon the face of the whole earth" (Gen 11:4). God goes "down" to intervene (Gen 11:6-8), with the result that the abandoned city "was called Babel, because there the LORD confused the language of all the earth" (Gen 11:9). The "Babelization" of language at the origins of human history are now confronted with another kind of speaking, that of the Word in the beginning before all human beginnings.[10] The words of the Word will promise both unity and true glory to those who receive him (John 12:32; 17:20-25). It is a God-given language since the Word will speak only what he has heard from the one who sent him (7:16; 12:49). In contrast to the attempt to mount to heaven by building a tower, John's gospel will present a lifting up of quite another kind (3:14; 8:28; 12:32).

10. This is not to suggest that the shifting contexts of theological language ever achieve a total expression of the Word. That would only replace the Babelized situation with the pretensions of logomania. In fact, the transcendence of the Word over all human words and contexts keeps the language of faith ever open to new possibilities of interpretation. See Joseph O'Leary, *La vérité chrétienne à l'âge, du pluralisme religieux* (Paris: Les éditions du Cerf, 1994), 81–90.

Something utterly decisive has occurred; it is suggested in the subtle change of tense in the use of the verb "to become."[11] Hence, the declaration: "What took place in him was life" (John 1:3b-4). In contrast to any understanding of the Word as an englobing cosmic presence, the focus shifts to an event within creation and its history. Where before all things came to be in the Word, now the Word comes to be within that universe.[12] A specific happening of the Word as the source and form of true life has occurred. The vitality of the Word will throw light on who God is, on what the world of creation is, and on the promise inherent in human destiny. The Word enters the flow of time as the embodiment of life and expands the meaning of creation in the radiance of light.[13] Existence now has a new vital energy at work within it and is illumined by a new meaning and direction. All of this has been made possible within creation in the happening of primordial life among us in the Word-become-flesh.

What, then, does the gift of "life" which happens in the Word add to that fact that all things were made in him? Another level of

11. The versatile Greek verb *ginomai* has many possible meanings. In John 1:3ab it refers to the *panta*, the "all things" of creation, in the aorist form of *egeneto*. The aorist form refers to a single act in the past, when "all things" came into being. But in its perfect form in v. 3c, *gegonen*, the reference is no longer to a past, once-only act of creation but to an act that happened *and continues* its influence into the present, namely, the "happening" of life and light in the incarnation.

12. For this interpretation of 1:3b-4, see Francis J. Moloney, *Belief in the Word: Reading John 1–4* (Minneapolis: Fortress Press, 1993), 30–34. For a magisterial overview of the Word's coming to be within the becoming and evolving universe, see Karl Rahner, "Christology within an Evolutionary View of the Word," in *Theological Investigations V*, trans. Karl-H. Kruger (Baltimore: Helicon, 1966), 157–92. Rahner's article can be read as a particularly effective transposition in an evolutionary worldview of Aquinas's words: "The mission of a divine person can be taken as implying, from one point of view, a procession of origin from the sender; and from another perspective, a new way of being in what is other. Thus the Son is said to be sent by the Father into the world, in that he begins to be in the world in the visibility of the flesh he has taken to himself" (*Summa Theol.*, I, q. 43, a. 1).

13. For an extended biblical and patristic meditation on the symbol of light, see Jaroslav Pelikan, *The Light of the World: A Basic Image in Early Christian Thought* (New York: Harper and Brothers, 1962).

relationship to God is implied. Through what has taken place, creation is made open to the original liveliness and vitality of God and the Word (John 1:1c). Creation can share in the Word's "being-turned" toward God in the beginning (1:1b), in receptivity and communion. The enlivening presence of the Word is utterly alien to the death-bound *bios* of an isolated and self-assertive existence, of a world closed in on itself.[14] In the coming of the Word, human existence is brought into the radiant field of its divine origin and God-ordained destiny.

Still, the gospel of the Word is neither theological information nor a contemplative escape from the drama of being in the world: "The light shines in the darkness, and the darkness has not overcome it" (John 1:5). The prologue recognizes the threat of an enveloping darkness and the impending realities of suffering and rejection. But the light continues to shine. In the interplay of the symbols of light and darkness, the evangelist depicts the luminous presence of the Word as the abiding source of Christian faith and hope. Nonetheless, there is a nondivine darkness that is somehow a counter-principle to the original being, life and light inherent in the divinely originated Word and in the origin of all things in him. The ruler of this world (John 16:11) is an agent of darkness and deception, organizing the world to reject its true life (cf. 1 John 2:15; 3:8), and the domain of the flesh is a chiaroscuro of countervailing influences. There is a struggle of light against a darkness blind to all that is truly of God. Though an inevitable conflict awaits the appearance of the Word, a serene confidence is expressed: "And the darkness has not overcome it" (1:5b). The conviction that light will continue to shine in an inextinguishable radiance suggests that the gospel is written out of an experience both luminous and liberating. Even at this early stage, the subversive light of the cross is intimated. The darkest moment of the world's rejection of the Word will be the hour when the glory of God's love will shine forth.

---

14. This point could be further developed in reference, from a Neo-Freudian perspective, to Ernst Becker, *The Denial of Death* (New York: Free Press, 1973), 47–66; and, in dependence on the anthropology of René Girard, Alison, *Raising Abel*, 29, 41–42, 58.

2. The Logos and Cosmos in Later Christian Theology

The Johannine prologue is not unlike a great classic poem as it invites to ever-deeper reflection while remaining inexhaustible in its potential range of reference. It draws the believer into a luminous space open to a horizon of limitless exploration. Within that space, Christian history has to keep trying to word the Word in ways that illumine the darkness of the successive eras of history. As the gospel unfolds, the Word, by becoming flesh, becomes a story, a conversation, a question, a theology, a prayer, and a promise—eventually a silence in the face of that death and resurrection before which all words must fail. But there are pauses in the conversation when the believing mind can recollect itself and pose new questions. How does such light illumine our planetary coexistence? How can such a culminating instance of God "so loving the world" (*kosmos* in the Greek) find new expression within the astonishing dimensions of the cosmos of our knowledge today?

It would be rather fundamentalist to expect to find in the New Testament instructions on modern ecological concerns or on, say, current cosmological scientific perspectives, for example, "the big bang." It is better, therefore, to emphasize the horizon or, to change the metaphor, the background radiation that shapes our sense of creation and the direction of its unfolding. The New Testament documents communicate not the conclusions we might reach in this much later age but open-ended ways of thinking and speaking suitable for integrating the range of each age's experience into the mystery of Christ.[15] In that regard, current scientific perspectives suggest a background against which the mystery of creation can be suggested—in all its complexity and unity.

Though this theological reflection concentrates on God's creative action in Christ, it feels no need to disregard or demean the activity of finite agencies in the genesis of the world.[16] God creates a world "in act"—in the complex relationality of atoms, neurons and DNA molecules, cells, organs, organisms, bodies, bondings, populations,

15. John F. Haught, *Christianity and Science: Toward a Theology of Nature* (Maryknoll, NY: Orbis, 2007), 109–34.

16. See Neil Ormerod, *Creation, Grace and Redemption* (Maryknoll, NY: Orbis, 2007), 3–44.

ecosystems, and the biosphere of this planet. Because God's infinite creative Act is involved in each of these activities, a higher possibility is anticipated in each step. Without such successive integrations, there would be no higher self-realization—no human existence, no incarnation, and no human minds and hearts aware of the creative Love of God.

One implication of a theology of creation is that the totality of reality must elude any exclusively scientific method, which such theology places in a larger field of human experience and exploration. Indeed, a religious sense of creation functions as a background theme in which all our diverse human creativities can improvise their variations as part of the symphony of reality. The scientist and philosopher Michael Polanyi generously observes:

> Admittedly, religious conversion commits our whole person and changes our whole being in a way that an expansion of our natural knowledge does not do. . . . It establishes a continuous ascent from our less personal knowing of inanimate matter to our convivial knowing of living beings and beyond this to knowing our responsible fellow men. Such I believe is the true transition from the sciences to the humanities, and also from our knowing the laws of nature to our knowing the person of God.[17]

Against this background, theology can seek to know more deeply "the person of God" in relation to the world. Given the cosmic tone of its primary sources—as in the prologue of John (1:1-18) and in Pauline writings (cf. Col 1:15-20; Eph 1:3-10)— Christian faith can hardly be deaf to the symphonic display of a creation centered on Christ. It can feel more keenly the need to articulate the cosmic significance of Christ at this present juncture of the history of Christian faith—which is now compelled to communicate with a world immeasurably more vast and intricate than what the ancients could have imagined and more disenchanted in terms of the religious sensibilities of past ages.

17. Michael Polanyi, "Faith and Reason," *Journal of Religion* 41 (1961): 244. For a fuller treatment, see his *Personal Knowledge: Towards a Post-critical Philosophy* (Chicago: University of Chicago Press, 1958).

3. New Rhetorics of Faith Expression

In its efforts to communicate with the world of today, Christians may profitably use three major arcs of rhetoric.[18] I use the word "rhetoric" in its classical sense, namely, the creative effort to bring experience to expression in the most telling way—in this case, faith's experience of the Word in the world of the day. The patterns of rhetoric referred to convey a distinctive sense of fulfillment, participation, and cosmic extension.

Fulfillment

The first rhetoric, then, deals with fulfillment: the Word incarnate fulfills the prayers and promises, the hopes and anticipations of the God-given dispensation that preceded him: "The law was given through Moses; the gift that is the truth came through Jesus Christ" (John 1:17). And from the perspective of the Letter to the Hebrews: "Long ago God spoke to our ancestors in many and various ways by the prophets, but in these last days, he has spoken to us by a Son" (Heb 1:1-2; NRSV). This kind of fulfillment is present primarily in the Scriptures as a fulfillment in history of the hopes of Israel awaiting its messianic deliverance and, beyond that, the hope that the good creation of God's original intention would reach fulfillment in the "Last Adam" (1 Cor 15:45).[19]

Later patristic theologies, such as those of Irenaeus of Lyons and Origen, would further explore the all-fulfilling role of Christ. The Scholastic theology of the Middle Ages, with its notion of Christ as

18. I owe this notion to the great ecumenical theologian Joseph Sittler, but with the passage of the years, the precise reference now eludes me. For a more specifically Pauline treatment of these issues, see the concise but stimulating work of Brendan Byrne, *Inheriting the Earth: A Pauline Basis of a Spirituality for Our Time* (Sydney: St Paul Publications, 1990).

19. *Adam,* in the biblical sense, is inclusive of all humanity. At first, *Adam* is the earth creature, shaped from the *adamah* (ground). Later, with the creation of woman, adamic experience becomes gendered. Through the creation of woman, *Adam* is transformed into *Ish* (a man) and *Ishah* (a woman). See Phyllis Trible, *God and the Rhetoric of Sexuality,* Overtures to Biblical Theology 2 (Philadelphia: Fortress, 1978), 94–98. Paul also expresses the inclusivity of being "in Christ" (Gal 3:28).

the perfect divine image, would set such a moment of fulfillment in a metaphysically determined universe. Even for the great Scholastics, however, the movement of history took place within a universe of fixed natures, a vertically arranged "chain of being," so to speak. Today the notion of a "fixed universe" has changed dramatically to an evolving, emerging cosmic process. The chain of being is horizontally linked, holding matter, consciousness, spirit together as ever-more complex phases of universal becoming. This new understanding of the universal process has enabled theology to present the mystery of Jesus Christ less in terms of the Word "coming down from heaven," or of God "sending his Son" into a fixed world of creation. The emphasis now is on God as the creative force enabling the continuous self-transcending process of the world, until it finally reaches the point of being able to receive the fullness of its originating mystery. In the consciousness of Christ, there is realized the moment of creation's acceptance of God as the ultimate dimension of its life, and the moment of God's acceptance of creation as personally God's own. Hence, Christ represents a decisive mutation offered to human consciousness. A new creation (2 Cor 5:17; Gal 6:15)—life to the full, a transformation of all things—has begun.

Participation

The second rhetoric is that of participation. It deals with our common connection in the reality of Christ: "in him was life" (John 1:4) and "from his fullness we have received" (John 1:16). He is the vine, we the branches (John 15:5f; cf. also John 14:6; Matt 11:27; Acts 4:12). The universal scope of God's creative intention is embodied in this man, Jesus: "I am the way, the truth and the life. No one comes to the Father except through me" (John 14:6). Contemporary theology explores our common participation in God's self-communication in Christ in new ways. Teilhard de Chardin, for example, sees Christ as the finality of creation already made present.[20] The whole meaning of the process of the world's continuing development is to incorporate all into the incarnate mystery of Christ. Every moment of time is impregnated with his presence. The whole cosmic process is Christ-bearing: "The prodigious expanses

---

20. For a good summary, see Haught, *Christianity and Science*, 66–84.

of time that preceded the first Christmas were not empty of Christ, for they were imbued with his power."[21] Material creation is not left behind, for it too finds its destiny by being incorporated into his transfigured Body: the whole of creation, physical and spiritual, is like a eucharistic host, offering itself to be consecrated and thereby transformed into the risen Lord.

Cosmic Expansion

The third rhetoric unfolds with a cosmic arc of reference. It elaborates the mystery of Christ in terms of universal expansion and inclusiveness: "all things were made through him, and without him nothing was made" (John 1:3; cf. Gen 1:1; Prov 8:27-30; Heb 1:2). Christ is the focus and extent of God's "so loving the world." In him is inscribed the meaning of the whole creation, for it is God's intention "to gather all things up in him, things in heaven and things on earth" (Eph 1:10; NRSV), just as he is "before all things, and in him all things hold together" (Col 1:17; NRSV). From these comprehensive perspectives, both protological and eschatological, there arise a variety of theologies centered on the Cosmic Christ.[22] The wider and deeper the dimensions of human experience, the richer the apprehension of the Christian mystery. Conversely, the more intimate our union with Christ, the more the "all" becomes a universe of grace.

Admittedly, the challenge today is to integrate into the intimacy and universality of faith not only the fourteen billion years of the world's emergence but also a capacity to cherish as God's creation the varied commonwealth of life in which we share. Whatever there is yet to occur in the world of our experience, whatever dimensions or dynamics there are in the cosmos of our present and further exploration, Christian faith must find its focus in him who is the consistency and coherence, the firstborn and the end of all creation. As Teilhard reminds us, "Christ must be kept as large as creation and remains its Head. No matter how large we discover the world to be,

---

21. Teilhard de Chardin, *The Hymn of the Universe* (London: Collins, 1970), 168.

22. See Denis Edwards, *Jesus and the Cosmos* (Mahwah, NJ: Paulist Press, 1991); also Jürgen Moltmann, *The Way of Christ: Christology in Messianic Dimensions* (London: SCM, 1990), 274–312.

the figure of Jesus, risen from the dead, must embrace it in its entirety."[23]

Such, then, is a brief outline of three fundamental arcs of Christian rhetoric. Each suggests a way of thinking, not only for New Testament authors, but also for theologians of every age. This is not to say that the creativity of the biblical trajectories was ever fully incorporated into later doctrinal councils and theologies. Official doctrines were limited to particular contexts. Creativity had to give place to other responsibilities. It should not be forgotten, however, that even the most austere doctrinal definition can be understood only as a more or less successful effort to objectify some dimension of Christian experience that was under threat. The full Christian fact resides in the whole life of the church. Doctrinal definitions emerge out of that life and return to it, to contribute the distinctive energy that precise clarification inspires. The liberation of the heart and the confident momentum of life cannot long endure without the creative and clarifying activity of intelligence.

4. Logos and Cosmos in a New Millennium

But whether we speak of the creative rhetoric of faith or the more precise articulations of belief regarding the incarnation of the Word in our world, Christian thought now faces an enormous challenge. As this third millennium unfolds, Christianity must rework its most basic understanding of creation in the light of the awe-inspiring dimensions of the world as they are emerging. The creation of the world and the divine coming-to-be within that world must now be meshed with an understanding of the manifold process of the world's emergence. The exploration of this self-transcending movement of creation in its relation to the self-communication of God remains one of the most energizing issues for Christian thinking in this new era.[24]

23. Cited in Christopher F. Mooney, *Teilhard de Chardin and the Mystery of Christ* (London: Collins, 1966), 136.

24. Though I have been speaking in classical terms of the incarnation of the Word, I do not mean to restrict this to the simple fact of the Word's becoming human. No Christian account of the meaning of the incarnation can pretend to

The classic doctrine of the flesh-taking of the Word was expressed by the Council of Chalcedon (451): "One and the same Son, Our Lord Jesus Christ . . . consubstantial with the father according to this divinity, consubstantial with us in his humanity." Within the horizon of human experience, the mystery of God and the reality of the human have come together in a unique, irreversible manner. God has communicated the God-self to the human, to be self-involved in its ultimate genesis. In Jesus Christ, the world is drawn into union with its original mystery. In him, that original mystery becomes part of the history of the world.

But, however eloquent its teaching, the universe envisaged in the Chalcedonian definition is quite limited. The implicit worldview is one of fixed, hierarchical arrangement. It is a cosmos of definable entities and intelligible order. It knows its problems and knows its needs. The chief among these is salvation and union with the absolute beyond all the fragmentation and flux of time. The One who is above comes to draw humankind into its own immortal and eternal sphere. The destiny of the human is to be divinized.

In contrast to such a worldview is that of contemporary science and culture. Hitherto unimaginable dimensions of time and space and energy have entered into our minds today. We understand and increasingly experience this world as one of amazing, intricate, and even chaotic emergence. It is a process, unfolding through billions of years in increasing differentiation of physical, chemical, and biological forms. It expresses itself in different and successive levels of organization: from the quantum behavior of particles to the formation of increasingly complex molecules to the emergence of life; from the protozoa to what we can now call plant, animal, and human. Such emergent differentiation and interiority, heading to the phenomenon of the human, dawns as a universe, a vast communion, a cosmic emergence already of unimaginable duration, begging for ever-more creative meanings to interpret it.

---

any completeness if it leaves out the actual life, passion, and death of Jesus, in his solidarity with the poor and the hopeless. Nor can we speak of the Light that is overcoming the darkness without referring to the resurrection, the final manifestation of the meaning of the Meaning, the *Logos*, uttered into hope's ongoing conversation.

How does the incarnation fit into such a scheme? How, why does God become human in such a cosmic unfolding? How is Christ incarnate, not only in an individual human body, but also in the cosmic body of emergent reality? These are the larger questions brought dramatically into consideration by the writings of Teilhard de Chardin. The divine appears more now as the limitless matrix of life out of which the whole process has emerged, to communicate itself in a personal way, in order to offer a new and final integration of the "all" in a common destiny.

And so, the great doctrinal inheritance of Chalcedon explodes into whole ranges of new questions. Perhaps they are best when most simply put: What if the incarnation were true? What difference would it make? What taste for life would it offer? What sense of the whole would it confer?

Without losing confidence in its basic affirmation, living much closer to the questionable, questing, wondering energies of faith can mean real gains for the vitality of Christian imagination. So, what if it were true that in Jesus of Nazareth the divine has expressed itself? What if it were true that the Word, the self-expression of limitless originating mystery, had become flesh, uttering itself into what seems most distant from any notion of the divine? What if it were true that the divine has uttered itself into the matter and processes, into the emergence, and into the community of this planetary life? What if it were true that the God, from whom the universe has come and is held in being, has become with us an earthling, to emerge out of the fertility of this process of life? What if it were true that the universe itself had become newly conscious of itself in the mind and heart of the Word made flesh, the Word incarnate, en-worlded, en-cosmified? What if it were true that the procession of the Word from the Father in the Spirit was the deepest structural dynamism of creation itself?

5. The Word and the Worlds of Meaning

But there are not only questions to be asked. New answers are also being shaped in both theology and the doctrinal expressions of faith—as in Vatican II's *Gaudium et Spes*. This seminal document gives expression to the cosmic, historical, social, and cultural understanding of human existence. One notes the change of emphasis, a readiness to employ a less philosophically burdened style of thinking. In many ways its language is a reversion to an earlier style of Christian thought characteristic of Irenaeus of Lyons and Origen and yet owing much to the influence of Teilhard and the evolutionary perspective of Karl Rahner. I feel it is important to take note of the meaning-making process that is in evidence in the creativity of the council's expression.

"Meaning" is a strange in-between kind of activity. By meaning something, we certainly intend to make a true statement. We are attempting to deal with reality. But that reality is disclosed only within a horizon lit by many kinds of meaning-full acts. To express the matter another way, it is not as though we simply put a meaning on things already somehow *there*. Rather, through our efforts to be meaning-making, we find our immersion in reality illuminated in seemingly endless ways. Without it, the world would be meaningless. For being human is a continuing effort to live in a meaning-full world, a world shot through with significance and intelligibility.

Cognitive Meaning

Without going into all the complexity of this topic, we usually associate meaning simply with what is meant in the world of known objects. Hence, the most noticeable function of meaning is that it orients us in an objective world. It is *cognitive*. This world of objects is one of limitless scope, from quarks to quasars, from photons to the world of faith, from protozoa to the Trinity itself. It is a world in which knowing supposes an increasing ability to name and to refer to a world of objects, in their distinctiveness and connections.

Now this has been very much the world of Christian faith with its hardy Greek intellectual inheritance. Theological systems characteristically endeavor to relate objects of faith to the world of science, philosophy, and the human sciences in general. Take the following passage, for instance, where the cognitive or objective meaning of Chalcedon's doctrine is being expanded and presented in fresh dimensions:

> The Word of God, through whom all things were made, was made flesh so that as perfect man he could save all human beings and sum up all things in himself. The Lord is the goal of human history, the focal point of the desires of history and

civilization, the center of humankind, the joy of all hearts, and the fulfillment of all aspirations. It is he whom the Father raised from the dead . . . constituting him judge of the living and the dead. Animated and drawn together in his Spirit, we press onward in our journey towards the consummation of history, which fully corresponds, to the plan of his love: "to unite all things in him, things in heaven, and things on earth" (Eph 1:10).[25]

The broader, more inclusive meaning of the incarnation contrasts with its comparatively isolated treatment in the classic definition of faith already referred to. In this regard, there is a more expansive objectivity in evidence.

At this point, we can introduce the presence of other more tacit and pervasive dimensions of Christian meaning. They serve to put the objective affirmations of the incarnation in a far richer field of reference. These three other dimensions of meaning are further ways of meaning reality and responding to its meaningfulness. There is *constitutive* meaning. It bears on our living sense of identity. Then there is *communicative* meaning. It establishes relationships of inclusion and belonging. A further range of meaning is *effective*. It changes things and in fact forms and even transforms our world. Let me illustrate each one in turn.

Constitutive Meaning

In addition to the cognitive meaning of the incarnation, there are other more interior, personal, and interpersonal dimensions of this event. Christian faith constitutes believers in a richer sense of human identity. It affects the manner we ultimately identify ourselves in a world created and assumed by God. Hence, to affirm that the Word became flesh and to mean it with the full assent of faith is obviously to mean something, but it is also to become someone in the process. The Christian is "in Christ," as St. Paul would say. Christian identity has been constituted within the universe of meaning and value so as to promote a distinctive *feel* for the universe, its origin, and its destiny.

---

25. *Gaudium et Spes* ("The Church in the Modern World"), par. 45, in *Vatican Council II: The Conciliar and Post Conciliar Documents*, ed. Austin Flannery (Northport, NY: Costello Publishing Co., 1992), 947.

Human consciousness is expanded and even transformed within a new realm of relationships such that the believer becomes a member of the Body of Christ, the temple of the Spirit, and enjoys a relationship of filial intimacy with God. To this degree, the manifold meaning of Christ informs consciousness and constitutes it in a new identity. The believer, through successive and more radical conversions, lives in a universe enfolded and energized by God's love. On the other hand, we may see ourselves merely as the tiniest of cosmic fragments or as a genetic link in the biological chain—perhaps lost in a blind and aimless evolutionary process. Still, faith, hope, and love can prevail, so that nothing "in all creation will be able to separate us from the love of God in Christ Jesus our Lord" (Rom 8:39; NRSV).

Believing in the incarnation is to participate in God's coming-to-be in the world of creation. Faith makes the heart intimate with this mystery that is at work. It inspires an atmosphere of hope in which the randomness, the chaos, the entropy of the physical universe is subsumed into the creativity of an ever-larger gift and an ever-greater Giver. Even sins and failures yield to the healing and forgiveness offered out of a limitless mercy.

Such a dimension of meaning is present in the following passage from *Gaudium et Spes* (my emphases):

> In reality, it is only in the mystery of the Word made flesh *that the mystery of the human truly becomes clear*. . . . Human nature by the very fact that it was assumed, not absorbed by him, has been raised in us also to a dignity beyond compare. For by his incarnation, he, the Son of God, has in a certain way, *united himself with every human being*. He worked with human hands, he thought with a human mind. He acted with a human will and loved with a human heart. Born of the Virgin Mary, he has been truly one of us, like to us in all things except sin. . . . All this holds true not for Christians only but also for all people of good will in whose hearts grace is invisibly active. For, since Christ died for all, and since in fact all are called to one and the same destiny, which is divine, we must hold *that the Holy Spirit offers to all the possibility* of being made partners, in a way known to God, in the paschal mystery.[26]

26. Ibid., par. 22.

More specifically, belief in the Word incarnate inspires a new sense of identity: "Life and death are made holy, and acquire a new meaning."[27] Human consciousness is informed with a sense of dignity and destiny within what can seem a threatening cosmos: "The riddle of suffering and death which, apart from the Gospel, overwhelms us."[28] The Word incarnate offers an intimacy with the universal Origin, for, through the gift of the Spirit, believers invoke the ineffable mystery with a filial familiarity, as they share in the identity of the Son: "We may cry out in the Spirit, 'Abba, Father!'"[29]

Communicative Meaning

Meaning is not only constitutive of identity but also communicative. Meaning functions not only by enabling us to mean *something* (cognitive), not only in making each of us a more meaningful *someone* (constitutive), but also as a communication in a field of meaning. It expresses a community of language, thought, feeling, ultimate purpose, and linked identity. At its most primitive and obvious, such a range of meaning is instanced as, say, when we can engage in conversation with someone. It is most noticeable in the formation of societies as they socialize their members into a particular way of life. In the ultimate horizon of belonging together, Christian faith communicates a rich range of community-forming meanings. It locates believers in the community of creation. It identifies them as members of the body of Christ. It promises a sharing in the "holy breath" of God and speaks of a common status as sons and daughters of God. This extension of meaning is well illustrated in the following words of Vatican II (my emphases):

> Just as God did not create human beings to live as individuals, but *to come together in the formation of social unity, so he willed to make them holy and to save them not as individuals without any bond or link between them but to make them into a people* who might acknowledge him and serve him in holiness. . . . This communitarian character is perfected and fulfilled in the work of Jesus Christ, for the Word made flesh willed to share in

27. Ibid.
28. Ibid.
29. Ibid.

> human fellowship. . . . As the firstborn of many brethren,
> by the gift of his Spirit, he established after his death and
> resurrection, *a new communion among all* who received him in
> faith and love; this is the communion of his own body, the
> Church, in which everyone, as members one of the other,
> would render mutual service in the measure of different gifts
> bestowed on each. *This solidarity must be constantly increased
> until that day when it will be brought to fulfillment*: on that day,
> humankind, saved by grace, will offer perfect glory to God as
> the family beloved of God and of Christ.[30]

The communicative dimension of meaning inspires a sense of
solidarity with others, in their sufferings, joys, and hopes. Today this
solidarity is extended in the grandeur of a shared scientific story of
our origins and of our genetic interconnection with other life forms
of the planet.[31] When the earth itself has become the symbol of the
one community of life, Christianity is invited to make deeper and
richer connections with the ground on which it stands, with the
nature in which it is immersed, with the cosmic body of its Lord.

Effective Meaning

Finally, there is the challenge to recognize more explicitly the effective dimensions of meaning. Meaning transforms the world. The
plans we make, the laws we enact, the moral norms we assent to, the
technologies we design, the priorities we assign, the skills we employ,
the cultural interests and political concerns we bring to any situation,
all conspire into a world-making and world-transforming energy.
Meaning makes the human world. Different kinds of effective bearing
of meaning are expressed, not only in the command to love our neighbor and to forgive our enemies, but also in the recent emphasis on
praxis in political and liberation theologies. These modes of Christian
thinking stress that, if the cognitive claims of Christian faith are to
mean something in the real world, if the identity it promises is to be
authentic, if the community it aspires to is going to be one of genuine

30. Ibid., par. 32.
31. For a fuller documentation of such communicative meaning, see Denis
Edwards, "The Integrity of Creation: Catholic Social Teaching in an Ecological
Age," *Pacifica* 5 (1992): 188–94.

solidarity, then its meaning must be effective. The test case of Christian meaning has typically been the genuine love of the neighbor. As this is extended into the whole neighborhood of creation in which our neighbors live, the effective scope of Christian meaning is expanded. The energies of love form the true face of the world. The "love [that] never ends" (1 Cor 13:8; NRSV) is the ultimately effective factor if the "fruits of our nature and our enterprise" are to be purified, illuminated, and transfigured:

> The Word of God, through whom all things were made, became human and dwelt amongst us: a perfect man, he entered world history, taking that history into himself and recapitulating it. He reveals to us that "God is love" (1 John 4:8) and at the same time teaches *that the fundamental law of human perfection, and consequently of the transformation of the world, is the new commandment of love.* [emphasis added][32]

The more the Word is en-fleshed in the world of human meaning, the more all the dimensions of meaning come into play in a mutually enriching manner. As the meaning of faith affirms the oneness of the universe in Christ, it illuminates the consciousness of being participants in a cosmic mystery of incarnation. It grounds a sense of inclusion in the one mystery of creation and inspires the transformation of the world itself. There occurs a circulation, even an "ecology," of Christian meaning as faith seeks to understand its truths, its consciousness, its community, the universe, and the Christian vocation in each age.

6. The Poem of the Word in the World

To summarize: our reflections on the *Logos* incarnate in the cosmos have dwelt on five considerations. First, drawing on the Johannine prologue (John 1:1-18), we considered how God's love for the universe is illumined by a recognition of the Word incarnate in creation. It radically affects human consciousness, for the *Logos* has entered the *dialogos* of the human conversation. Second, we touched

---

32. *Gaudium et Spes*, par. 38.

upon the significance of John's theology of the incarnate Word in later Christian theology. Third, we noted three arcs of rhetoric in the expression of faith, in its effort to word the Word in the world of our experience. Fourth, we proceeded to consider how the meaning of the incarnation, expressed in its classical doctrinal form, now confronts Christians in a new millennium with new kinds of questioning. Finally, we indicated four dimensions of meaning in which this fundamental mystery is presently being expressed in church doctrines. A multidimensional Christian meaning orders, suffuses, connects, and orients our experience of the mystery of Christ. Teilhard de Chardin writes: "Throughout my life, by means of my life, the world has little by little caught fire in my sight until, aflame all around me, it has become almost completely luminous from within. . . . Such has been my experience in contact with the earth—the diaphany of the divine at the heart of the universe on fire. . . . Christ; his heart, a fire: capable of penetrating everywhere and gradually spreading everywhere."[33]

These brief pointers only suggest the dimensions of the great challenge confronting Christian thinking, but also provoke a rereading of the past. The work of Irenaeus of Lyons and Origen are often instanced. But even in the work of such an adversarial and logical thinker as Tertullian, precious resources awaiting a larger retrieval are in evidence. To give one precious example: "Think of God utterly taken up with the task of creation, with hand, sense, industry, forethought, wisdom, providence, and, above all, with that loving care which was determining the features. For the image of Christ, the man who was to be, was influencing every stage in the molding of the clay; because what was at that moment happening to the earth's clay, would happen again when the Word became flesh."[34]

When all is said and done, it is a matter of appreciating anew the Word incarnate, precisely as Word, who comes from the divine Artist as a great Poem. The sublimity of the hymnic prologue of John, referred to at the beginning of this chapter, points in that direction.

---

33. Teilhard de Chardin, *The Divine Milieu* (New York: Harper Torchbooks, 1960), 46n1.

34. Quoted in Gabriel Daly, *Creation and Redemption* (Dublin: Gill and Macmillan, 1988), 77.

The Word, the *Logos*, the Meaning incarnate, works in human consciousness as a great poem. As Les Murray, himself a remarkable poet, has stated:

> Religions are poems. They concert
> our daylight and our dreaming mind, our
> emotions, instinct, breath and native gesture.[35]

Murray's words remind us that the manifold meanings of faith are carried, not primarily in words or concepts, but in the pulse and momentum of our living. The incarnation transforms our taste for reality, our whole feel for life as it carries us on. Its meaning is inexhaustible, for

> Full religion is the large poem in loving repetition;
> like any poem, it must be inexhaustible and complete
> with turns where we ask, Now why did the poet do that?[36]

In the interests of "full religion," or at least of a fuller version of it, we have been involved in a kind of "loving repetition" within the new contexts of our concern. And there are certainly those turns where we are left with a question for the divine Poet of the Word. While that Word draws us into a vision of all things held in existence, illumined and linked in the event of incarnation, there are moments of utter darkness, taking us to the depths of human tragedy, into the silence of the tomb when the incarnate Word is a tortured corpse. But we are not left there. No cosmic "black hole" of meaninglessness has swallowed him. There is that "white hole," if that is not too banal a parallel, of life transformed, of resurrection, disclosing a new and final form of existence. There, the fragmented and groping meanings of faith come home, and what is obscure and unfinished on this side of darkness blazes with light.

---

35. Les Murray, "Poetry and Religion," in *Blocks and Tackles: Articles and Essays 1982–1990* (Sydney: Angus and Robertson, 1990), 172.
36. Ibid., 172.

Bibliography

Aasgaard, Reidar. "Paul as a Child: Children and Childhood in the Letters of the Apostle." *JBL* 126 (2007): 129–59.

Alexander, Philip S. "Targum, Targumim." In *The Anchor Yale Bible Dictionary*, edited by David N. Freedman. Vol. 6:320–31. New York: Doubleday, 1996.

Alison, James. *Raising Abel: The Recovery of Eschatological Imagination*. New York: Crossroad, 1996.

Amery, Carl. *Das Ende der Vorsehung. Die gnadenlosen Folgen des Christentums*. Reinbek: Rowohlt, 1972.

Anderson, Bernhard W. "Exodus Typology in Second Isaiah." In *Israel's Prophetic Heritage: Essays in Honor of James Muilenburg*, edited by Bernhard W. Anderson and Walter J. Harrelson, 177–95. New York: Harper & Brothers, 1962.

Aquinas, Thomas. *St Thomas Aquinas Summa Theologiae*. Translated by Thomas Gilby. Vol. 5. Cambridge, UK: Blackfriars, 1967.

———. *St Thomas Aquinas Summa Theologiae*. Translated by T. C. O'Brien. Vol. 14. Cambridge, UK: Blackfriars, 1975.

Athanasius of Alexandria. *Letters to Serapion*. Translated in Khaled Anatolios, *Athanasius*. The Early Church Fathers. London and New York: Routledge, 2004.

———. *On the Incarnation*. Translated in R. W. Thompson, *Athanasius, Contra Gentes and de Incarnatione*. Oxford: Clarendon Press, 1971.

———. *Orations against the Arians*. Translated in Khaled Anatolios, *Athanasius*. The Early Church Fathers. London and New York: Routledge, 2004.

Bailie, Gil. *Violence Unveiled: Humanity at the Crossroads*. New York: Crossroad, 1997.

Barbour, Ian G. *When Science Meets Religion: Enemies, Strangers or Partners?* New York: HarperCollins, 2000.

Barton, John. "Reading the Prophets from an Environmental Perspective." In *Ecological Hermeneutics: Biblical, Historical and Theological Perspectives*, edited by David Horrell, et al., 46–55. London: T&T Clark International, 2010.

Bauckham, Richard. *Bible and Ecology: Rediscovering the Community of Creation*. London: Darton, Longman & Todd, 2010.

———. *God and the Crisis of Freedom: Biblical and Contemporary Perspectives*. Louisville, KY: Westminster John Knox Press, 2002.

———. "Joining Creation's Praise of God." *Ecotheology* 7 (2002): 45–59.

Beale, G. K. *The Temple and the Church's Mission: A Biblical Theology of the Dwelling Place of God*. New Studies in Biblical Theology 17. Downers Grove, IL: InterVarsity Press, 2004.

Beauchamp, Paul. "Création et fondation de la loi en Gen, 1:1-2, 4." In *La Création dans l'orient ancient*, edited by F. Blanquart, 139–82. Paris: Cerf, 1987.

Becker, Ernst. *The Denial of Death*. New York: Free Press, 1973.

Beker, Johan C. *Paul the Apostle: The Triumph of God in Life and Thought*. 2nd ed. Philadelphia: Fortress Press, 1984.

Berry, Robert James, ed. *Environmental Stewardship: Critical Perspectives—Past and Present*. New York: T&T Clark International, 2006.

Blenkinsopp, Joseph. *Creation, Un-Creation, Re-Creation: A Discursive Commentary on Genesis 1–11*. London: T&T Clark, 2011.

———. *Isaiah 40–55*. Anchor Bible 19a. New York: Doubleday, 2002.

Boismard, Marie-Émile, and Arnaud Lamouille, eds. *L'évangile de Jean*, Synopse des quatre evangiles en Français 3. Paris: Cerf, 1977.

Botterweck, G. Johannes, and Helmer Ringgren, eds. *Theological Dictionary of the Old Testament*. 14 vols. Grand Rapids, MI: Eerdmans, 1974.

Bourdieu, Pierre. *Contre-feux 2. Pour un mouvement social européen*. Paris: Raisons d'Agir, 2001.

Brady, Augustine. "Martin Buber and the Gospel of John." *Thought* 201 (1978): 283–92.

Braudel, Fernand. *The Mediterranean and the Mediterranean World in the Age of Phillip II*. Vol. 1. Berkeley: University of California Press, 1996.

Brown, Francis, S. R. Driver, and Charles A. Briggs, eds. *A Hebrew and English Lexicon of the Old Testament*. Oxford: Clarendon Press, 1977.

Brown, Jeannine K. "Creation's Renewal in the Gospel of John." *CBQ* 72 (2010): 275–90.

Brown, William P. *Ethos of the Cosmos: The Genesis of Moral Imagination in the Bible*. Grand Rapids, MI: Eerdmans, 1999.

———. *The Seven Pillars of Creation: The Bible, Science, and the Ecology of Wonder*. Oxford: Oxford University Press, 2010.

Brueggemann, Walter. *Isaiah 40–55*. Louisville, KY: Westminster John Knox Press, 1998.

Bultmann, Rudolf. "Ursprung und der Typologie als hermeneutischer Methode." *TLZ* 75 (1950): cols. 206–12.

Burge, Garry H. *The Anointed Community: The Holy Spirit in the Johannine Community.* Grand Rapids, MI: Eerdmans, 1987.

Byrne, Brendan. *Inheriting the Earth. The Pauline Basis of a Spirituality for Our Time.* Homebush, Australia: St Paul Publications, 1990.

———. *Romans.* Sacra Pagina 6. Collegeville, MN: Liturgical Press, 1996.

Childs, Brevard. *Introduction to the Old Testament as Scripture.* Philadelphia: Fortress Press, 1979.

Christensen, Michael J., and Jeffery A. Wittung, eds. *Partakers of the Divine Nature: The History and Development of Deification in the Christian Tradition.* Grand Rapids, MI: Baker Academic, 2007.

Coad, Dominic. "Creation's Praise of God: A Proposal for a Theology of Non-Human Creation." *Theology* 112 (2009): 181–89.

Coloe, Mary L. " 'The End Is Where We Start From': Afterlife in the Fourth Gospel." In *Lebendige Hoffnung—Ewiger Tod?! Jenseitsvorstellungen Im Hellenismus, Judentum Und Christentum. (Living Hope—Eternal Death?! Conceptions of the Afterlife in Hellenism, Judaism and Christianity)*, edited by Manfred Lang and Michael Labhan, 177–99. Leipzig: Evangelische Verlagsanstalt, 2007.

———. *God Dwells with Us: Temple Symbolism in the Fourth Gospel.* Collegeville, MN: Liturgical Press, 2001.

———. "The Nazarene King: Pilate's Title as the Key to John's Crucifixion." In *The Death of Jesus in the Fourth Gospel*, edited by Gilbert Van Belle, 839–48. Louvain: KUL Press, 2007.

———. "Raising the Johannine Temple (John 19:19–37)." *ABR* 48 (2000): 47–58.

———. "The Structure of the Johannine Prologue and Genesis 1." *ABR* 45 (1997): 1–11.

Conradie, Ernst M. "The Road towards an Ecological Biblical and Theological Hermeneutics." *Scriptura* 93 (2006): 305–14.

———. "What on Earth Is an Ecological Hermeneutics? Some Broad Parameters." In *Ecological Hermeneutics: Biblical, Historical and Theological Perspectives*, edited by David G. Horrell, et al., 295–315. London: T&T Clark International, 2010.

Cooper-White, Pamela. *The Cry of Tamar: Violence against Women and the Church's Response.* Minneapolis: Fortress Press, 1995.

Daly, Gabriel. *Creation and Redemption.* Dublin: Gill and Macmillan, 1988.

de Chardin, Teilhard. *The Divine Milieu.* New York: Harper Torchbooks, 1960.

———. *The Hymn of the Universe.* London: Collins, 1970.

Dillard, Annie. *Pilgrim at Tinker Creek.* New York: HarperPerennial, 1974.

Drinkard, Joel F., Jr. "East." In *The Anchor Yale Bible Dictionary*, edited by David N. Freedman, 248. New York: Doubleday, 1992.

Driver, Samuel R. *An Introduction to the Literature of the Old Testament*. 9th ed. Edinburgh: T&T Clark, 1913.

Dunn, James D. G. *Romans 1–8*. Word Biblical Commentary. Vol. 38A. Dallas: Word Books, 1988.

Earth Bible Team. "Conversations with Gene Tucker and Other Writers." In *The Earth Story in Genesis*, edited by Norman C. Habel and Shirley Wurst. The Earth Bible 2, 21–33. Sheffield, UK: Sheffield Academic Press, 2000.

———. "Guiding Ecojustice Principles." Chap. 2 in *Readings from the Perspective of Earth*, edited by Norman C. Habel. The Earth Bible 1. Sheffield, UK: Sheffield Academic Press, 2000.

Edwards, Denis. *How God Acts: Creation, Redemption and Special Divine Action*. Hindmarsh, Australia: Australian Theological Forum, 2010.

———. "The Integrity of Creation: Catholic Social Teaching in an Ecological Age." *Pacifica* 5 (1992): 188–94.

———. *Jesus and the Cosmos*. Mahwah, NJ: Paulist Press, 1991.

———. "Teilhard's Vision as Agenda for Rahner's Christology." *Pacifica* 23 (2010): 233–45.

Edwards, Ruth. " 'Charin anti Charitos' (John 1:16): Grace and the Law in the Johannine Prologue." *JSNT* 32 (1988): 3–15.

Egan, Harvey. "Theology and Spirituality." In *The Cambridge Companion to Karl Rahner*, edited by Declan Marmion and Mary E. Hines, 13–28. Cambridge, UK: Cambridge University Press, 2005.

Eliade, Mercia. *The Sacred and the Profane: The Nature of Religion*. New York: Harcourt, Brace & World Inc., 1959.

Ferguson, Niall. *Civilization: The West and the Rest*. New York: Penguin Press, 2011.

Feuerbach, Ludwig. *The Essence of Christianity*. Translated by George Elliot. New York: Cosimo Classics, 2008.

Feuillet, André. *Johannine Studies*. Staten Island, NY: Alba House, 1964.

Finch, Jeffrey. "Athanasius on the Deifying Word of the Redeemer." In *Theōsis: Deification in Christian Theology*, edited by Stephen Finlan and Vladimir Kharlamov, 104–21. Cambridge, UK: James Clarke & Co, 2006.

Finlan, Stephen, and Vladimir Kharlamov, eds. *Theōsis: Deification in Christian Theology*. Cambridge, UK: James Clarke & Co, 2006.

Fishbane, Michael. *Biblical Interpretation in Ancient Israel*. Oxford: Clarendon Press, 1985.

Fitzmyer, Joseph. A. "The Letter to the Romans." In *The New Jerome Biblical Commentary*, edited by Raymond E. Brown, Joseph A. Fitzmyer, and Roland E. Murphy, 832–68. London: Geoffrey Chapman, 1990.

―――. "Pauline Theology." In *The New Jerome Biblical Commentary*, edited by Raymond E. Brown, Joseph A. Fitzmyer, and Roland E. Murphy, 1382–1416. London: Chapman, 1990.

Flannery, Austin, ed. *Vatican Council II. The Conciliar and Post Conciliar Documents*. Northport, NY: Costello Publishing Co., 1992.

Flood, Josephine. *Archaeology of the Dreamtime: The Story of Prehistoric Australia and Its People*. Pymble, Australia: Angus and Robertson, 1992.

Foerster, Werner. "Εἰρήνη." In *Theological Dictionary of the New Testament*, edited by Gerhard Kittel, Geoffrey William Bromiley, and Gerhard Friedrich, 2:412–15. Grand Rapids, MI: Eerdmans, 1964–76.

Fretheim, Terence E. *God and World in the Old Testament: A Relational Theology of Creation*. Nashville, TN: Abingdon Press, 2005.

―――. "Nature's Praise of God in the Psalms." *Ex Auditu* 3 (1987): 16–30.

Gammage, Bill. *The Biggest Estate on Earth—How Aborigines Made Australia*. Sydney: Allen & Unwin, 2011.

Gardner, W. H., and N. H. MacKenzie, eds. *The Poems of Gerard Manley Hopkins*. 4th ed. Oxford: Oxford University Press, 1970.

Geertz, Clifford. "Thick Description: Towards an Interpretive Theory of Culture." In *The Interpretation of Cultures: Selected Essays*, edited by Clifford Geertz, 3–33. New York: Basic Books, 1973.

Gnuse, Robert K. *Heilsgeschichte as a Model for Biblical Theology: The Debate concerning the Uniqueness and Significance of Israel's Worldview*. College Theological Society. Lanham, MD: University Press of America, 1989.

Goldingay, John. *The Message of Isaiah 40–55: A Literary-Theological Commentary*. London: T&T Clark, 2005.

Gordon, Robert P., ed. *The God of Israel*. University of Cambridge Oriental Publications 64. Cambridge, UK: Cambridge University Press, 2007.

The Green Bible. New York: HarperOne, 2008.

Groth, A. Nicholas, and H. Jean Birnbaum. *Men Who Rape: The Psychology of the Offender*. New York: Plenum Press, 1979.

Habel, Norman C. *The Earth Story in the Psalms and Prophets*. The Earth Bible 4. Sheffield, UK: Sheffield Academic Press, 2001.

―――. "Geophany: The Earth Story in Genesis 1." In *The Earth Story in Genesis*, edited by Norman C. Habel. Sheffield: Sheffield Academic Press, 2000.

Haught, John F. *Christianity and Science: Toward a Theology of Nature*. Maryknoll, NY: Orbis, 2007.

Hayman, Peter. "Rabbinic Judaism and the Problem of Evil." *SJT* 29 (1976): 461–76.

Hays, Robert B. *The Moral Vision of the New Testament*. Edinburgh: T&T Clark, 1997.

Henderson, Ebenezer. *The Book of the Prophet Isaiah*. London: Hamilton Adams & Co., 1840.

Hengel, Martin. "The Old Testament in the Fourth Gospel." In *The Gospels and the Scriptures of Israel*, edited by Craig Evans and W. Richard Stegner, 380–95. JSNTSup 104. Sheffield, UK: Sheffield Academic, 1994.

Hermission, Hans Jürgen. *Studien zur Prophetie und Weisheit*. Tübingen: Mohr Siebeck, 1998.

Hooker, Morna. *Endings: Invitations to Discipleship*. Peabody, MA: Hendrickson, 2003.

Horrell, David G. *The Bible and the Environment: Towards a Critical Biblical Ecological Theology*. London: Equinox, 2010.

Horrell, David G., Cherryl Hunt, and Christopher Southgate, "Appeals to the Bible in Ecotheology and Environmental Ethics: A Typology of Hermeneutical Approaches." *SCE* 21 (2008): 219–38.

Horrell, David G., Cherryl Hunt, Christopher Southgate, and Francesca Stavrakopolou, eds. *Ecological Hermeneutics: Biblical, Historical and Theological Reflections*. London: T&T Clark, 2010.

Hoskyns, Edwyn C. "Genesis I–III and St John's Gospel." *JTS* 21 (1920): 210–18.

Jastrow, Marcus. *A Dictionary of the Targumim, the Talmud Babli and Yerushalmi, and the Midrashic Literature*. New York: Judaica Press Inc. 1975.

Johnson, Elizabeth. *She Who Is: The Mystery of God in Feminist Theological Discourse*. New York: Crossroad, 1992.

Johnson, Luke Timothy. *Reading Romans: A Literary and Theological Commentary*. New York: Crossroad, 1997.

Kasper, Walter. *The God of Jesus Christ*. London: SCM, 1983.

Kelly, Anthony J., and Francis J. Moloney. *Experiencing God in the Gospel of John*. Mahwah, NJ: Paulist, 2003.

King, Philip J., and Lawrence E. Stager. *Life in Biblical Israel*. London: Westminster John Knox Press, 2001.

Koch, Klaus. "Ugaritic Polytheism and Hebrew Monotheism in Isaiah 40–55." In *The God of Israel*, edited by Robert P. Gordon, 205–28. University of Cambridge Oriental Publications 64. Cambridge, UK: Cambridge University Press, 2007.

Küng, Hans. *Does God Exist? An Answer for Today*. Translated by Edward Quinn. New York: Vintage Books, 1981.

Labuschagne, Casper J. *The Incomparability of Yahweh in the Old Testament*. Pretoria Oriental Series 5. Leiden, Netherlands: Brill, 1966.

Landy, Francis. *Paradoxes of Paradise. Identity and Difference in the Song of Songs*. Sheffield, UK: The Almond Press, 1983.

Larsen, David K. *God's Gardeners: American Protestant Evangelicals Confront Environmentalism, 1967–2000*. University of Chicago PhD, 2001.

Lee, Dorothy A. "Beyond Suspicion? The Fatherhood of God in the Fourth Gospel." *Pacifica* 8 (1995): 140–54.

———. *Flesh and Glory: Symbolism, Gender and Theology in the Gospel of John*. New York: Crossroad, 2002.

Lewis, Charlton T., and Charles Short. *A Latin Dictionary*. Oxford: Clarendon Press, 1922.

Liddell, Henry G., and Robert Scott, eds. *An Intermediate Greek -English Lexicon*. Oxford: Clarendon Press, 1896.

Lines, William J. *A Long Walk in the Australian Bush*. Sydney: University of New South Wales, 1999.

Louth, Andrew. *Maximus the Confessor*. London: Routledge, 1996.

Lovelock, James. *The Ages of Gaia: A Biography of Our Living Earth*. Oxford: Oxford University Press, 1998.

———. "The Fallible Concept of Stewardship of the Earth." In *Environmental Stewardship: Critical Perspectives—Past and Present*, edited by R. J. Berry, 106–11. London: T&T Clark, 2006.

———. *The Revenge of Gaia: Why the Earth Is Fighting Back—and Why We Can Still Save Humanity*. London: Allen Lane, 2006.

Lowenthal, David. *The Past Is a Foreign Country*. Cambridge, UK: Cambridge University Press, 1985.

Lucas, Alec J. "Reorienting the Structural Paradigm and Social Significance of Romans 1:18-32." *JBL* 131 (2012): 121–41.

Macquarrie, John. *Jesus Christ in Modern Thought*. London: SCM Press, 1990.

Maher, Michael. *Targum Pseudo Jonathan: Genesis*. The Aramaic Bible. Vol. 1b. Collegeville, MN: Liturgical Press, 1987.

Maier, Harry O. "Green Millennialism: American Evangelicals, Environmentalism and the Book of Revelation." In *Ecological Hermeneutics: Biblical, Historical and Theological Reflections*, edited by David G. Horrell, Cherryl Hunt, Christopher Southgate, and Francesca Stavrakopolou, 246–66. London: T&T Clark, 2010.

Mann, Thomas W. "Guest Editorial," *Interpretation* 65 (2011): 337–39.

Manns, Frédéric. *L'evangile de Jean à la lumière du Judaïsme*. Studium Biblicum Franciscanum Analecta 33. Jerusalem: Franciscan Printing Press, 1991.

Marlow, Hilary. *Biblical Prophets and Contemporary Environmental Ethics: Re-reading Amos, Hosea and First Isaiah*. Oxford: Oxford University Press, 2009.

Moldenke, Harold M., and Alma L. Moldenke. *Plants of the Bible*. London: Routledge, 2002.

Moloney, Francis J. *Belief in the Word. Reading John 1–4*. Minneapolis: Fortress Press, 1993.

———. *The Gospel of John*. Edited by Daniel J. Harrington. Sacra Pagina 4. Collegeville, MN: Liturgical Press, 1998.

Moltmann, Jürgen. *The Way of Christ: Christology in Messianic Dimensions*. London: SCM, 1990.

Mooney, Christopher F. *Teilhard de Chardin and the Mystery of Christ*. London: Collins, 1966.

Moore, Megan Bishop, and Brad E. Kelle. *Biblical History and Israel's Past: The Changing Study of the Bible and History*. Grand Rapids, MI: Eerdmans, 2011.

Muraoka, Takamitsu. *A Greek-English Lexicon of the Septuagint*. Louvain: Peeters, 2009.

Murray, Les. "Poetry and Religion." In *Blocks and Tackles: Articles and Essays 1982 to 1990*. Sydney: Angus and Robertson, 1990.

Murray, Robert. *The Cosmic Covenant: Biblical Themes of Justice, Peace and the Integrity of Creation*. London: Sheed & Ward, reprinted 2007.

Neuner, Josef, and Jacques Dupuis, eds. *The Christian Faith in the Doctrinal Documents of the Catholic Church*. London: Collins Liturgical, 1982.

North, Christopher R. *The Second Isaiah: Introduction, Translation and Commentary to Chapters XL–LV*. Oxford: Clarendon Press, 1964.

O'Leary, Joseph. *La vérité chrétienne à l'âge, du pluralisme religieux*. Paris: Les editions du Cerf, 1994.

Ormerod, Neil. *Creation, Grace and Redemption*. Maryknoll, NY: Orbis, 2007.

Peacocke, Arthur. *God and the New Biology*. London: J. M. Dent and Sons, 1986.

Pelikan, Jaroslav. *The Light of the World: A Basic Image in Early Christian Thought*. New York: Harper and Brothers, 1962.

Plaut, W. G., ed. *The Torah*. New York: Union of American Hebrew Congregations. 1981.

Polanyi, Michael. "Faith and Reason." *Journal of Religion* 41 (1961): 237–47.

———. *Personal Knowledge*. Chicago: University of Chicago Press, 1958.

Pound, Ezra. *ABC of Reading*. New York: New Directions, 2010.

Purdum, Todd S. "From That Day Forth," *Vanity Fair* (February 2011): 105.

Rahner, Karl. "Christology in the Setting of Modern Man's Understanding of Himself and of His World." In *Theological Investigations* 11, translated by David Bourke, 215–29. New York: Seabury Press, 1974.

———. "Christology within an Evolutionary View of the Word." *In Theological Investigations* 5, translated by Karl-H. Kruger, 157–92. Baltimore: Helicon, 1966.

———. *Foundations of Christian Faith: An Introduction to the Idea of Christianity.* Translated by William V. Dych. New York: Seabury Press, 1978.

———. *Hominisation: The Evolutionary Origin of Man as a Theological Problem.* Translated by W. J. O'Hara. London: Burns and Oates, 1965.

———. "Immanent and Transcendent Consummation of the World." In *Theological Investigations* 10, translated by David Bourke, 281–89. London: Darton, Longman & Todd, 1973.

———. "Resurrection: D. Theology." In *Encyclopedia of Theology: A Concise Sacramentum Mundi,* edited by Karl Rahner, 1440–42. London: Burns and Oates, 1975.

Rogerson, John. "The Creation Stories: Their Ecological Potential and Problems." In *Ecological Hermeneutics: Biblical, Historical and Theological Perspectives,* edited by David G. Horrell, et al., 21–31. London: T&T Clark International, 2010.

Rolston, Holmes. *Science and Religion: A Critical Survey.* 1987. Reprint, Philadelphia and London: Templeton Foundation Press, 2006.

Rosik, Mariusz. "Discovering the Secrets of God's Garden: Resurrection as New Creation (Gen 2:4b–3:24; John 20:1–18)." *Studium Biblicum Franciscanum: Liber Annuus* 58 (2009): 81–98.

Santmire, H. Paul. *Nature Reborn: The Ecological and Cosmic Promise of Christian Theology.* Minneapolis: Fortress Press, 2000.

———. *The Travail of Nature: The Ambiguous Ecological Promise of Christian Theology.* Philadelphia: Fortress Press, 1985.

Schama, Simon. *Landscape and Memory.* London: Fontana Press, 1996.

Schillebeeckx, Edward. *Church: The Human Story of God.* New York: Crossroad, 1990.

———. *For the Sake of the Gospel.* New York: Crossroad, 1990.

Schnackenburg, Rudolf. *The Gospel According to St John.* Translated by K. Smyth, et al. Herder's Theological Commentary on the New Testament. 3 vols. London: Burns & Oates, 1968–82.

Schneiders, Sandra M. "The Lamb of God and the Forgiveness of Sin(s) in the Fourth Gospel." *CBQ* 73 (2011): 1–29.

———. "The Resurrection (of the Body) in the Fourth Gospel." In *Life in Abundance: Studies of John's Gospel in Tribute to Raymond E. Brown,* edited by John R. Donahue, 168–98. Collegeville, MN: Liturgical Press, 2005.

Schweizer, Eduard. "Σάρξ." In *Theological Dictionary of the New Testament,* edited by G. Kittel, G. W. Bromiley, and G. Friedrich. Vol. 7, 98–151. Grand Rapids, MI: Eerdmans, 1964.

Sherwin, Simon J. "Old Testament Monotheism and Zoroastrian Influence." In *The God of Israel,* edited by Robert P. Gordon, 113–24. University of Cambridge Oriental Publications 64. Cambridge, UK: Cambridge University Press, 2007.

Shiva, Vandana. "Let Us Survive: Women, Ecology and Development." In *Women Healing Earth*, edited by Rosemary Radford Reuther, 65–73. Maryknoll, NY: Orbis Books, 1996.

Silverman, Jason. *Persia and Apocalyptic: The Transition from Prophecy to Apocalyptic in Second Temple Judaism* (PhD thesis, Trinity College, Dublin, 2011).

Simmons, J. Aaron. "Evanelical Environmentalism: Oxymoron or Opportunity?" *Worldviews: Religions, Culture and Ecology* 13 (2009): 40–71.

Smith, Morton S. *The Origins of Biblical Monotheism: Israel's Polytheistic Background and the Ugaritic Texts*. Oxford: Oxford University Press, 2001.

Sommer, Benjamin D. *A Prophet Reads Scripture: Allusion in Isaiah 40–66*. Stanford, CA: Stanford University Press, 1998.

Southgate, Christopher. *The Groaning of Creation: God, Evolution and the Problem of Evil*. Louisville, KY: Westminster John Knox Press, 2008.

Stager, Lawrence E. "Jerusalem as Eden." *Biblical Archaeology Review* 26, no. 3 (2000): 36–47.

Stanner, William E. H. *The Dreaming and Other Essays*. Melbourne: Black Ink Agenda, 2009.

Stockton, Eugene. *The Aboriginal Gift*. Alexandria, Australia: Millennium Books, 1995.

Suggit, John N. "Jesus the Gardener: The Atonement in the Fourth Gospel as Re-Creation." *Neotestamentica* 33 (1999): 161–68.

Thomas, Robert L. "שָׁלֵם, Shalem." In *New American Standard Hebrew-Aramaic and Greek Dictionaries: Updated Edition*, H7999. Anaheim, CA: Foundation Publications, 1998.

Thompson, Marianne Meye. *The God of the Gospel of John*. Grand Rapids, MI: Eerdmans, 2001.

Thunberg, Lars. *Man and the Cosmos: The Vision of Maximus the Confessor*. Crestwood, NY: St Vladimir's Seminary Press, 1985.

Tracy, David. *The Analogical Imagination: Christian Theology and the Culture of Pluralism*. London: SCM, 1981.

———. *Pluralism and Ambiguity. Hermeneutics, Religion, Hope*. San Francisco: Harper and Row, 1987.

Trible, Phyllis. *God and the Rhetoric of Sexuality*. Overtures to Biblical Theology 2. Philadelphia: Fortress, 1978.

Wallace, Howard N. "Eden, Garden of (Place)." In *The Anchor Yale Bible Dictionary*, edited by David N. Freedman. Vol. 2. New York: Doubleday, 1992.

————."Garden of God (Place)." In *The Anchor Yale Bible Dictionary*, edited by David N. Freedman. Vol. 2. New York: Doubleday, 1992.

Weinfeld, Moshe. "God the Creator in Genesis 1 and in the Prophecy of Second Isaiah." *Tarbiz* 37 (1967–68): 105–32; 123–24 [Hebrew].

Weingreen, Jacob. *A Practical Grammar for Classical Hebrew*. 2nd ed. London: Clarendon, 1959.

White, Lynn, Jr. "The Historical Roots of Our Ecological Crisis." *Science* 155, (1967): 1203–7.

Witherington III, Ben. *John's Wisdom: A Commentary on the Fourth Gospel*. Louisville, KY: Westminster John Knox, 1995.

————. "The Waters of Birth: John 3.5 and 1 John 5.6-8." *NTS* 35 (1989): 155–60.

Zimmermann, Ruben."Symbolic Communication between John and His Reader: The Garden Symbolism in John 19–20." In *Anatomies of Narrative Criticism: The Past, Present, and Future of the Fourth Gospel as Literature*, edited by Tom Thatcher and Stephen D. Moore, 221–35. Society of Biblical Literature Resources for Biblical Study 55. Leiden, Netherlands: Brill, 2008.

Zohary, Michael. *Plants of the Bible*. Cambridge, UK: Cambridge University Press, 1983.

Author Index

Aasgaard, R., 61
Alexander, P. S., 25
Alison, J., 96, 99
Amery, C., 34
Anderson, B. W., 50
Aquinas, T., 8, 9, 10, 94, 98
Athanasius, 4, 5, 11, 15, 87, 88, 89, 90

Bailie, G., 96
Barton, J., 38
Bauckham, R., 2, 53, 54
Beale, G. K., 83
Beauchamp, P., 22, 23
Becker, E., 99
Beker, J. C., 67, 68
Berry, R. J., 52
Blenkinsopp, J., 42, 43, 49, 75, 87
Boismard, M-É., 77
Bourdieu, P., 54
Brady, A., 94
Braudel, F., 36
Brown, J. K., 81, 82
Brown, W. P., 42, 47, 48, 49
Brueggemann, W., 41, 49
Bultmann, R., 45
Burge, G. H., 86
Byrne, B., 60, 61, 62, 102

Childs, B., 42
Christensen, M. J., 89
Coad, D., 55
Coloe, M. L., ix, 64, 71, 72, 74, 84
Conradie, E. M., vii, 37
Cooper-White, P., 21

Daly, G., 114
de Chardin, T., 89, 90, 103, 104, 105, 107, 108, 114, 120, 124
Dillard, A., 16
Driver, S. R., 20, 39
Dunn, J. D. G., 62

Edwards, D., vii, 1, 87, 89, 90, 104, 112
Edwards, R., 74
Egan, H., 6, 7
Eliade, M., 54

Ferguson, N., 34
Feuerbach, L., 41
Feuillet, A., 3
Finlan, S., 89
Fishbane, M., 47
Fitzmyer, J. A., 67, 87
Flood, J., 29, 30
Fretheim, T. E., 20, 21, 54

Gammage, B., 20, 30, 31
Geertz, C., 45
Gnuse, R. K., 45
Goldingay, J., 46
Gordon, R. P., 39, 46
Groth, A. N., 21

Habel, N. C., vii, viii, 21, 28, 29, 54
Haught, J. F., 100, 103
Hayman, P., 46
Hays, R. B., 51
Henderson, E., 39
Hengel, M., 78. 86
Hermission, H. J., 50
Hooker, M., 72, 86
Hopkins, G. M., 22, 32
Horrell, D. G., vii, 19, 34, 35, 37, 38, 53, 55, 56
Hoskyns, E. C., 80, 81, 82, 87

Johnson, E., 16
Johnson, L. T., 58

Kasper, W., 11, 12, 15, 16
Kelly, A. J., vii, 91
Koch, K., 39
Küng, H., 41

Labuschagne, C. J., 39
Landy, F., 65, 66
Larsen, D. K., 51
Lee, D. A., 74, 80
Lines, W. J., 54
Lovelock, J., 52, 54
Lowenthal, D., 36

Macquarrie, J., 91
Maier, H, O., 35
Manns, F., 77, 81, 84
Marlow, H., 37
Moldenke, H. M., 48

Moloney, F. J., 73, 74, 91, 92, 98, 122
Moltmann, J., 104
Mooney, C. F., 105
Moore, M. B., 36
Murray, L., 115
Murray, R., 51

Neuner, J., 93
North, C. R., 39, 42, 46

O'Leary, J., 97
Ormerod, N., 100

Pelikan, J., 98
Polanyi, M., 101

Rahner, K., 5, 6, 7, 9, 10, 11, 77, 89, 90, 98, 108
Rogerson, J., 18, 22
Rolston, H., 17
Rosik, M., 82, 83

Santmire, H. P., 18, 34
Schama, S., 42, 54
Schillebeeckx, E., 13, 14
Schnackenburg, R., 88
Schneiders, S. M., 58, 59, 69, 88
Sherwin, S. J., 46
Shiva, V., 21
Silverman, J., 46
Simmons, J. A., 51
Smith, M. S., 39
Sommer, B. D., 47
Southgate, C., 17, 35
Stager, L. E., 36, 83
Stanner, W. E. H., 29, 30
Stockton, E., 29
Suggit, J. N., 88, 89

Thompson, M. M., 74
Thunberg, L., 95

Tracy, D., 94
Trible, P., 102

Wallace, H. N., 83
Weinfeld, M., 47

White Jr., L., 19, 34, 35, 36, 52, 56
Witherington III, B., 77, 80

Zimmermann, R., 81, 82, 85
Zohary, M., 48